NARCISSISM

Learn How to Identify, Disarm, and Protect Yourself From Narcissists, Sociopaths, Psychopaths

(Healing From the Manipulation of the Covert Narcissism)

Melody Bancroft

Published by Kevin Dennis

Narcissism: Learn How to Identify, Disarm, and Protect Yourself From Narcissists, Sociopaths, Psychopaths (Healing From the Manipulation of the Covert Narcissism)

ISBN 978-1-989920-27-5

Legal & Disclaimer

The information contained in this book is not designed to replace or take the place of any form of medicine or professional medical advice. The information in this book has been provided for educational and entertainment purposes only.

The information contained in this book has been compiled from sources deemed reliable, and it is accurate to the best of the Author's knowledge; however, the Author cannot guarantee its accuracy and validity and cannot be held liable for any errors or omissions. Changes are periodically made to this book. You must consult your doctor or get professional medical advice before using any of the suggested remedies, techniques, or information in this book.

Upon using the information contained in this book, you agree to hold harmless the Author from and against any damages, costs, and expenses, including any legal fees potentially resulting from the application of any of the information provided by this guide. This disclaimer applies to any damages or injury caused by the use and application, whether directly or indirectly, of any advice or information presented, whether for breach of contract, tort, negligence, personal injury, criminal intent, or under any other cause of action.

You agree to accept all risks of using the information presented inside this book. You need to consult a professional medical practitioner in order to ensure you are both able and healthy enough to participate in this program.

Table of Contents

Introduction

In our fast-paced, impersonal world, we all need to love ourselves a little.

We need to find some worth within us, to believe that we are capable of loving and being loved. We need to know we have a reasonable chance of achieving our goals and making our way through the maze of life's challenges.

But what happens when our view of ourselves becomes totally distorted from reality? What happens when we falsify who we are and create an image that, while grand and important, has no root in reality?

We may be treading on the quicksand of narcissism, a mental disorder.

We fall off the edge of a healthy self-confidence and into a world of exaggerated self-importance. The line between our fantasy world and our real world blurs.

Unchecked, we can progress to Narcissistic Personality Disorder where we admire ourselves so much we can summon only contempt for others. Our whole world becomes compromised. We cannot build and enjoy lasting relationships, our work life is endangered and we become angry and stressed at a world that just doesn't measure up to our high demands. In some cases, suicidal thoughts can occur.

Narcissism and Narcissistic Personality Disorder should concern everyone, especially for those who experience the symptoms and those who view them in others. That is because it is a growing problem in developing countries throughout the world, particularly in youthful populations.

Unlike any previous time in history, we are seeing increased numbers of people experiencing symptoms of Narcissistic Personality Disorder and the unhappiness that accompanies it.

The trend first appeared on the horizon in 2008 when researchers at the National Institutes of Health discovered that almost 10 per cent of Americans in their 20s had experienced some form of the disorder in their lives.

The study, published in the **Journal of Clinical Psychiatry,** supported other research conducted at American universities. Another study, that included 35,000 Americans of all ages, indicated that one out of every 16 people had experienced what they described as clinical Narcissistic Personality Disorder during their lives.

If you find yourself exaggerating your achievements when you discuss yourself with friends and new acquaintances, if you day-dream constantly about being honored for your power, brilliance or beauty, if you honestly believe that you are superior to everyone around you, and if you don't mind taking advantage of other people to get what you want, you are already exhibiting narcissistic tendencies.

If you are envious of other people and require constant attention and admiration, you are also in danger of letting narcissism lead you down a dark road in life.

The good news is that if caught early, narcissistic tendencies can be stemmed. You can bring yourself back from the brink with home remedies and a designated plan of action.

In advanced cases, clinical therapy is effective.

Narcissism is not a personality disorder that needs to be treated with medications or massive change. Rather, for most people, a conscious plan for small changes can restore balance in your personality. Talk therapy programs with trained professionals also have yielded good results.

This book explores the whole idea of how much we love ourselves and when we cross over into the land of too much.

We have combed all the recent scientific studies published in peer-reviewed journals and brought them together in straightforward terms so you fully comprehend all the aspects of narcissism and Narcissistic Personality Disorder.

In the coming chapters we will show you how to:
- Determine if you are exhibiting the signs of narcissism and Narcissistic Personality Disorder
- Illustrate the impact of an exaggerated sense of self-worth on your ability to relate to others
- Study the difficulties of being or working with a narcissist in the workplace
- Help you to see the world from the perspective of other people
- Delve into the narcissist's inability to apologize
- Examine why we pretend to be more important than we are
- Explore the darkest sides of narcissism such as rage and contempt at everyone around you

6

- Calculate the true cost of using other people to advance your own agenda

We will also discuss why we all need a certain amount of narcissism to lead healthy lives.

Finally, we will look at the reasons why narcissism as a personality disorder is on the rise in our current culture and the factors that are fueling its growth.

Whether you are living with someone who suffers from narcissism or whether you recognize yourself as someone sliding in that direction, this book is an intriguing read into a personality disorder that was identified generations ago, but is more prevalent in our modern world than ever before.

Chapter 1: Understanding Narcissism

A narcissist is a person who has a personality disorder in which he or she is excessively preoccupied with dominance, power, prestige, and vanity. They do not realize the destruction they cause to themselves and others. A so-called narcissist can do things without noticing the feelings of the people around them. They consider themselves truly superior and they need to be respected. You can call them vain or selfish, those are just some of the common labels used by many towards narcissists. They are involved in feelings, as for them it's only normal to feel hurt. They came up with this **narcissist** version of themselves so that it can serve as the shock absorber.

However, a narcissistic pain is different from other types of emotional pain.

People who suffer from narcissism often display attitudes like being snobbish, patronizing or even disdain. For example, he or she may complain about a bartender's rudeness or stupidity or conclude a medical evaluation with a condescending evaluation of the physician.

A personality disorder is a kind of pattern and behavior that deviates from the norm individual's culture. This pattern is seen in the following areas: cognition; interpersonal functioning; impulse control; or affect. The enduring pattern is not exactly flexible and it can also be seen at one's early childhood characteristics. The pattern is stable and is in long duration.

Narcissism is more prevalent in males than females. However, as time passed by and when they suppress all the feelings, this disorder is to decreased and symptoms become lesser at the age of the 40s to 50s.

There are things that cause a person to become a narcissist. Researchers today don't exactly know what causes a person to eventually turn into a narcissist. There are many theories, however, only about the possible cause of narcissistic personality disorder.

Most professionals subscribe to a bio-psychosocial model of causation – that is, the cause of are likely due to biological and genetic factors, social factors, such as how people react to one another starting from their early age up to the present. Consider the psychological factors, which are the personality and temperaments of a human being shaped by the environment and the learned coping skills to deal with stress. This suggests that there is no single factor responsible in becoming a narcissist – rather, it is the complex and likely intertwined nature of all factors that are important. If a person has this personality disorder, they are suggested to become a carrier of it and pass it down to their unknowing children.

There are actually treatments of this personality disorder, which typically involves long-term psycho treatment or psychotherapy, with a therapist who has a wide experience in treating this kind of personality disorder. Some medications can actually help with specific sets of symptoms. The person with this kind of disorder usually exaggerate things around him, they also tend to have a daydreaming about fantasies of beauty, success and power over dominating their thoughts. This type of person is also too sensitive. They need to be admired in everything they do at all times. If not, they will be hurt deep inside.

They also tend to manipulate and take advantage of the people around them using their emotional feelings that people around them needs to consider, as a weapon. They lack empathy that makes us feel and recognize the feelings of needs of others. These types of people also are the envy type ones and their behavior appears to us as haughty or arrogant.

A person with untreated Narcissistic Personality Disorder has a higher chance of substance abuse including drugs and alcohol, depression, problems with a relationship, difficulties at work or school and suicidal behaviors or thoughts. Recent studies found out that males with narcissism have higher measures of **cortisol** in their blood. **Cortisol** is a stress hormone, so basically this disorder is caused by too much stress triggered by experience from childhood up to the point where they cannot handle it anymore.

Even those who do not have so much stress have higher levels of **cortisol**. High levels of **cortisol** is linked to a greater risk of developing some kind of heart problems. Family members of somebody with this disorder describe the sufferer as controlling and forever dissatisfied with what anybody around them does. The narcissist will never fail blame others and make them feel guilty of their problems and what they are into now. They are described as short and ill tempered. They lose their tempers at the slightest provocation and think that every little thing is not going their way. They will think that people around them always turns their backs and gives them a silent treatment.

Worst cases can turn a human being to someone who is very abusive both physically and sexually. Living with a narcissist can feel as if you're living a very confusing nightmare. It's like you are getting into jail with a no exact way of escape. The spouse, co-workers, boss, and even the parent can sometimes get stuck in a relationship they find very hard to escape from. The emotional and the physical damages caused by somebody with the disorder can be severe. Health care professionals aren't an exception to emotional exhaustion.

Narcissists strive to defend their fragile self-esteem through the use of facade and carefully produced blind spots in their thinking. Living in a fantasy world, where they meet all their needs and unrealistic expectations take the place of life. They feel superior with this wonderland that they made up in their heads without noticing the effects they are making to the people around them. They become involved in beauty, material things, and shallowly develop interest in things that are not real such as soap operas, movies, games, and rock stars.

They fear their feelings. They cannot gain and keep a deep friendship or intimacy and cannot develop a mature love relationship. A fantasy world can be a sweet escape for a narcissist and can also become an attempt not to see what is really there in order to build up self-esteem. Narcissist people process information, emotions, and unresolved pain to make up for their hidden damaged childhood. They love achieving something with their own imaginations in their created world and they often place an unrealistic demand to someone else just to feel better. They are not one to tolerate negative emotional distress, as they are not very good at it. They usually push it to others and blame them instead of looking closer to see their own part of the problem. This is the defense of projection – when a certain person does not like him or herself, they get angry to those who have some of the likable traits.

The Self-image is distorted in narcissistic point of view and the person believes that he is more superior than others. An over the top self-esteem is a defense to cover up the unforgettable shame deep within. Grandiosity is an insidious error in thinking that it is a prevention and it stops them from blaming themselves and becoming depressed or disintegrated.

Narcissist people like to hear the sound of their own voice. They are individuals that thrive on being the center of attraction and attention who tends to put down others whom they feel is inferior. At work, a narcissist is power hungry and will go to great lengths to gain power. Learning if you are with a narcissist can be quite difficult and confusing in the sense that you also might be confused about what you feel towards the narcissist you are with.

Narcissists prefer to work under their own set of rules. Narcissist only cares about themselves and therefore, when working with a narcissist, always remember that they will never be a great buddy to be with. They will befriend you to convert you into one of their victims or supply sources, will do favors expecting a big return and you will do the same thing as well to them. Unfortunately, in the workplace you can't just do anything that you want to this person and walk away without so much as an issue. So the best thing to do is to go along with him or her. Getting in touch with a narcissist more often will keep them from thinking you don't like them. But be careful of getting too close with a narcissist because they think different and digest words from you differently. Narcissist do expect you to be immediately responsive the moment they demand attention just like a normal boss in your company who wants you to immediately follow him in everything he demands.

Sharing your emotions to a narcissist is a big no because you are forcing them to prioritize your feelings. The next best thing that you can actually do is focus on solutions and not the problem. Narcissist likes to focus on the problem and turn it over, around, rearrange, and practically dissect it to pieces. They tend to make things very complicated. Stop looking at the glass as if it is half empty. The best thing that you can do is flip it and influence the narcissist to see the other side of truth.

It's actually a good choice to just present several solutions. Narcissist likes to be in control and they'd love you if you have this much-favored ability to offer them options. This is one of the several ways that you can make them feel as if you truly respect their opinion and that you are asking them to take control and show you what they are made of. If it still does not work out, you best last option is to make them feel good about themselves, unique, and special. Narcissists wants to be praised and they like the feeling that they are higher than you. They get high off of being in power and they thrive in attention and admiration. If you want them to be happily productive for you, simply let them know how great they are. Praising them makes them feel at peace.

When a narcissist grows up, they harbor the irrational belief that the person they choose as a partner will give them perfect love and make up for all hurts and slights of their life. This burning desire for getting unconditional love is an unresolved need from their damaged childhood. While most adults find the good thing about unconditional, understand also that it rarely happens. This is because the people we love usually holding us somehow responsible for our actions. Think carefully about imposing your neediness and bad behavior towards others.

Being a narcissist is not an easy thing, people with this kind of disorder don't need to be rejected and taken for granted. They believe that everything is fine because that's the way they grew up with, which is a normal thing for them. People with this kind of disorder need more attention and understanding, no one wishes to be born with this disorder. People with a narcissistic behavior have a sense of entitlement that allows them to break the rules of society. They believe that laws do not apply to them and they do not feel remorse when they get caught. However, they are upset over any inconveniences they suffer as a result of being busted. They believe they have the right to do whatever it takes to get short term gratification without suffering any consequences.

Narcissism in Everyday Life

We have already defined narcissism, but how does it relate to normal everyday life? To have a better understanding of narcissism, let us look at a fictional character Tom.

Tom is a regional cooperate manager. At first glance, he is a gem. He seems pleasant, charming, and endearing; all the traits you would expect from someone in his position. However, the moment you get to know Tom more, you start to realize some things that may not necessarily seem charming. Tom hates it when you contradict him in meetings, either at work or social settings. He is not as open to suggestion as you might believe. He thinks his opinions are of utmost importance, and for this reason, he expresses them freely without any consideration for anyone else. He may ask for your opinions but at this stage it is only a formality and not something he would devote his attention to. He hates challenges, he is unsure of winning, and loathes criticism. He acts as if he is a demigod who deserves worship. He wants his words to be considered regarded as the Gospel and there is no argument beyond that. If he is kept waiting, or things do not go according to what he deems to be the correct way, in this case his way, he can blow things out of proportion. Throwing tantrums or delving into an extremely unpleasant behavior is easy for such a person. He will hold grudges against people who stand up to him, regardless of whether they were right or not. This behavior is downright childish and is also not the only childish behavior he will exhibit. As a man who is used to getting his way, at restaurants, he is the person who must get the table he wants at the snap of a finger. When he does not get the table, or the service he wants, he is quick to throw an anger fit. For these reasons, Tom has no real friends. His self-inflated ego and sense of importance gradually throw him out of favor of almost all his acquaintances. Although he has a downright charming persona and a general gentlemanly attitude, all of it falls apart slowly as you get to know him more. Everyone who gets to know him eventually gets tired of him and his godlike, self-centered attitude. Due to his self-centeredness, he has difficulty connecting with people, as well as being sensitive to their needs or wants. Do not get me wrong, Tom helps a few people, but only when it casts him in a positive light or advances his own personal agenda. It is also debatable that Tom does not consider himself friends with anybody. As far as he is concerned, he owes a few people a few favors. He sees people as resources rather than friends. He uses them to get his will done.

For Tom, there is no separation from his self-righteousness. For this reason, his wife, children, and neighbors find it difficult to communicate with him as well as live with him because he expects everybody to agree with his opinions. Tom is a narcissist through and through. And getting him to admit this will prove to be an uphill task. I am not saying Tom is a bad person. He might have a misplaced sense of self-righteousness that may seem absolutely right to him but is heavily flawed from another perspective. He may never realize this because the only perspective he is willing to consider is his own. If his wife is not a quiet woman, he is extremely likely to end up quarrelling with her often for petty reasons. A family life for such a person may be harder to maintain than for normal people. As a parent, his communication with the kids will be heavily one sided.

As I have said, narcissism, to some degree, is healthy. Confidence and solid faith in one's abilities is sometimes misinterpreted as narcissism. Confidence or over confidence can sometimes be considered arrogance but it is almost never a narcissistic trait. There are many confident people in the world; people who believe in themselves and their abilities. Absolute faith in one's abilities cannot be summarized as narcissism. The only difference between these people and a pathological narcissist is that unlike the narcissist, they do not consider themselves a cut above the rest (better than anyone) or demand that they be accorded special treatment. They do not insist that they stand above their peers and deserve special treatment. They are more devoted to the job or the task at hand. A confident and strong-willed individual is more likely to be successful than a narcissist. While a narcissist doles away admiring himself the confident person gets the job done.

This is not to mean that they do not consider themselves the best in their field of study; no, they simply are not envious or harbor any grudge against other accomplished people in the same field of study as them. They are aware of their needs and feelings as well as those of people around them. They do not think that every opportunity to help someone else is an opportunity to advance their own agenda. They genuinely care about others. The narcissistic individual on the other hand is the opposite. He looks for loopholes and ways to divert every opportunity in his favor regardless of its impact on the people around him. Jealousy and peer rivalry might also induce him to drag down the people he envies. A narcissist may even go so far as to refuse helping a colleague who works in the same field of study that he does. All out of hatred for that person!

Here are some of the main characteristics a pathological narcissist will display.

1. They always feel entitled, as if everything is their right.
2. They are constant attention-seekers who desire admiration most times.
3. They are exploitive. They will take advantage of a child if it will advance their self-centered agenda.
4. If your suffering or distress will not advance his or her agenda, then it is of little concern to them. They are unable to identify with any feeling or emotion that is not helpful to the attainment of their agenda.
5. Jealousy is their middle name. When someone else gets the prize instead of him or her, he or she will be envious and feel like it should have been him or her.
6. They are extremely arrogant.

7. They are preoccupied with dreams of grandeur, unlimited success, beauty,

ideal love, and marriage. They believe that their brilliance is comparable to Albert Einstein's.

Chapter 2: Narcissistic Personality Disorder – Causes, Diagnosis And Treatment

Causes

There has been a lot of research into what causes narcissistic personality disorder but researchers are still unable to answer the question. There are theories though and many professionals believe that the causes are most likely to be a combination of genetic, social and biological factors. This includes looking at how a person with narcissistic personality disorder interacted with other people, like friends and family, in their early years. They also include psychological factors such as what sort of personality the individual has, what their temperament is like and how they cope with stress.

The suggestion is that narcissistic personality disorder cannot be put down to one single factor, rather it is a highly complex and entwined combination of factors and, research does show that, where a person suffers from narcissistic personality disorder, their children have a higher risk than normal of having it as well.

Diagnosis

A diagnosis for any personality disorder must be made by a professional trained in mental health. This usually means that a psychiatrist or psychologist must make the diagnosis, not the family GP. General practitioners are not trained in mental health procedures and, while it is possible to consult one initially, they should then refer the individual to a properly trained professional.

Professional diagnoses are not made using blood tests, lab test or any kind of genetic test. Most people who have narcissistic personality disorder will not actively seek out treatment because they do not believe there is anything wrong with them. They would rather believe that everyone else around them needs to seek treatment before they do. In general, most people with any personality disorder will not seek any kind of help until the disorder interferes with their lives in a way that it can no longer be ignored. This usually happens when coping skills are stretched to the point of snapping and the individual can no longer deal with stress or any other event in their lives.

A professional will make a diagnosis of narcissistic personality disorder by looking at your symptoms and your life history and comparing them to those listed above. They will determine if any or all of your symptoms match those that are required for a diagnosis of narcissistic personality disorder.

Treatment

Treatment involves psychotherapy and is a long-term treatment plan. It must be done by a suitably qualified and experienced therapist and, in conjunction with a doctor; they may also prescribe medication to help with specific symptoms. Treatment plans are specific to the individual and, as such, we cannot give you an overview, as it wouldn't be accurate enough.

Chapter 3: Why Do Narcissists Abuse People They Love?

One of the most outright difficult questions that you have to tackle when you decide to study something as dense and challenging as narcissism is the question of why people with narcissistic personality disorder abuse the people that they love. The trouble with narcissistic personality disorder is that it isn't as clear-cut as we would like for it to be. In the chapter following this one, we're going to outline a lot more about what goes on with a narcissistic person and how you can use that information in order to both identify someone who most likely has narcissistic personality disorder as well as how the information comes in handy in terms of knowing if you're caught in a cycle of abuse.

For now, though, we're just going to try to get a clearer understanding of what is going on in the brain of somebody who is narcissistic, as well as analyzing what this information has to do with somebody's general behavior towards people that they love. This can be a bit of a difficult puzzle to piece together, so I ask that you bear with me as we try to make sense of this mess of a personality disorder.

The first thing that you need to understand about narcissistic personality disorder is that there is no singular cause. The cause appears to be a unified combination of things ranging from genetics to one's environment to one's upbringing. One also needs to understand that it doesn't seem to manifest in any singular uniform way. There are so many ways for narcissistic personality disorder to manifest, in fact, that psychologists and psychiatrists have determined up to eleven different subtypes of this disorder, all behaving in unique yet tangentially related ways.

In the first chapter, we discussed narcissism in a very bare way and laid out what narcissistic personality disorder is at its core. What we didn't discuss at very great length was what exactly narcissistic personality disorder is in terms of a person's actions. While we're going to save the majority of the discussion of symptoms for the next chapter, we do need to go beyond the definition of "self-obsession" for a moment.

We first need to establish that the basis of narcissistic personality disorder lies in the fact that a person not only desires but needs and thrives on the validation and acceptance of others. That is to say that a person who has narcissistic personality disorder feels that they must be accepted by others and seen as some image of greatness that they perceive themselves as.

In understanding this phenomenon, we can start to understand the concept of validation in narcissism a bit more. Mainly, we can use this as a jumping off point in order to start discussing why a person might behave like they do. The understanding of validation serves as an essential starting point to the understanding of why somebody with narcissism might abuse somebody that they love.

It's also important to note that not all narcissism is borne from the same reasoning. We discussed this bit a moment ago, but we're going to dive into it a bit deeper now: narcissism mainly has two root social causes. The first is that the person was under-praised, harshly criticized, or even suffered from some sort of emotional abuse as a child. In this case, the development of narcissistic personality disorder mainly served as a defense mechanism so that they wouldn't believe terrible things about themselves, acting as a method to block out the negativity and perhaps as a subconscious knee-jerk response to the emotional depth and vitriol they were forced to deal with.

The second cause is that the person was over-praised or otherwise validated in some central way by people who were important to them, such as parents or peers, without any sort of actual evidence in order to back up the level of praise that was rendered. This made the person in question feel exceptional while they were developing leading to them having grandiose visions of themselves and their abilities.

So, how does all of this play into somebody's patterns of abuse? Basically, with these two extremely different causes—causes which are, more or less, polar opposites. You need to understand that one way or another, the narcissist deeply craves validation from their partner or victim. It's unfortunate, but they really do thrive off of validation such that they subconsciously need it or else they will react in a knee-jerk way to the lack of validation, which often is rendered as emotional abuse, anger, general irritability, or either real or faux depression.

Another important thing to understand about the narcissistic patterns of abuse lies in the fact that narcissism is often comorbid with other extremely strenuous personality disorders. After all, most personality disorders have similar root causes as subconscious reactions in response to external stresses. These simultaneously acting personality disorders may be things such as borderline personality disorder or histrionic personality disorder, both of which serve to either end up with the extreme over- or undervaluation of partners and general figures in life, leading to an inevitably unsteady and often abusive relationship.

In understanding why people with narcissistic personality disorder choose to abuse their partners, it's also important to understand that many narcissists are only exhibiting learned behavior that they internalized as okay from a figure such as a father or a mother. Failure to realize behavior as unhealthy ultimately led to them accepting the behavior as a perfectly fine way to act. It, of course, is **not** a perfectly fine way to act, but the narcissist doesn't know any better and, at this point in their development, doesn't have the capacity to care either.

So really what i'm trying to say is that if a narcissist abuses their partner, there's a pretty decent chance that they themselves were abused by a narcissist in their lives. They then internalized this sort of behavior as acceptable and normal and then express themselves through that action in their own relationships. This isn't serving as a means to rationalize what they're doing or humanize them at all—abuse, in general, is absolutely grotesque and devastating. However, it does give one the ability to understand in a general sense why one might behave in the way that they do.

In the end, people serve one primary use to the narcissist: the validation of their own personality and the facade that they set up for themselves. A narcissist will find a person useful insofar as they are able to fulfill this purpose, and failure to fulfill this purpose will often lead to frustration on the narcissist's part.

The combination of the desire for intense validation and the need for admiration with the generally ingrained negative behavior patterns of the narcissist combines to create the perfect storm for a heavily unhealthy relationship based around validation, a lack thereof, and an incredible amount of underlying tension.

It's easy to ask the question: does the narcissist love me? While we are going to get into that question a bit more in-depth a little bit later, it's hard to answer on its own because the answer is a bit difficult to give. Understand that regardless of the narcissist's feelings for you, you ultimately simply serve as a part of their toolbox for self-validation.

However, this doesn't mean in and of itself that they don't or cannot love you. One thing you need to understand about narcissistic personality disorder is that despite the fact that they may feel capacity for love, the part of their brain which has to do with empathy is quite literally shrunken in most cases, which means that even if they can love, they don't feel the same amount of empathy that a neurotypical human being would. This can be a huge cause of stress in your relationship and lead to them not understanding why certain things that they do are fundamentally incorrect in a moral sense.

Do understand, though, that any extant love isn't a validation of the way that they may act towards you. There are a great many reasons that a narcissistic person may act abusively towards a person that they love. This does not, however, serve to make any of the reasons fundamentally correct or even relatively acceptable. They are not acceptable, flatly, and you ultimately deserve better than abuse— nobody deserves abuse.

It takes a lot of honesty with oneself to attempt to understand why somebody who has narcissistic personality disorder may choose to abuse the people that they love because it's immensely difficult to leave any sort of structure, especially if there's an abuse component to it. Your mind is actively working against you in these sorts of scenarios, so understanding that a person may be abusive and not the right sort of environment to be within is absolutely vital.

Chapter 4: How To Tell If You're With A Narcissist

EXCESSIVE CHARM

The Narcissist at first meeting is an enigmatic, charismatic charmer who will sweep you off your feet.

He's funny. He makes you laugh. He talks to you non stop (mostly about himself).

Not just attentive, but mega-attentive, fixing you with his eyes and blatantly touching you. He seems to be totally obsessed with you and you begin to feel that there must be a chemistry between you.

There will be compliments galore and, as the relationship progresses, over the top grandiose displays of affection (huge bouquets sent to you at work for example). Calling you at all times of the day or next, texting, emailing. He has to be in touch with you. When can he see you again?

If you are honest with yourself though, the "wooing" stage does feel a little weird and uncomfortable.

Some of it is embarrassing, especially in front of friends or when he calls you at work and won't get off the line. Attention is nice though and the Amorous Narcissist has scoped you out long enough to know that your lonely, heartbroken, wounded or vulnerable. He knows what you want and is giving it to you in spades. So you ignore your fears. You tell yourself it's about time you had someone in your life who genuinely loves you.

The intensity of his gaze is not romantic interest, its scanning your facial movements, the look in your eye, assessing how your reacting to his advances and adjusting accordingly. He asks you questions or comments on subjects in order to find out which subject is the weak spot for you so that he can puncture that area with his vampire fangs.

You are not the love of his life, you are prey!

ARROGANCE

This is not confidence. You will think it is at first. But the narcissist just loves himself so much and can see no reason why he shouldn't say so.

He will over exaggerate his achievements and brag about them to you. He will build up such a picture of perfection that you will think all your dreams have come true. He's rich. He has a great job and will one day be a partner because he has made so much money for that company. He has a ton of friends who would do anything for him. His family is perfection and he can't wait for you to meet them (which doesn't seem to happen). His academic prowess knows no bounds. Women adore him and he has to turn them down constantly. He is a pillar of the community, a respected member of the church, incredibly good looking and an all round great guy. You do realise how lucky you are to get him don't you?

Nobody is so self assured in all aspects of life. Someone may be confident at work or athletically or in their appearance, but nobody feels that they have it all.

I once knew a Narcissist who went for a job interview and told the Interviewer that he could make their company great and if they employed him they would make a fortune! This, however, had no previous experience and hadn't worked for 2 years! Needless to say he didn't get the job. But who does that? The Narcissist believes that stuff about himself. He is awesome and surely everyone can see that? When he didn't get the job the Narcissist blamed the person he had asked for a reference, saying he had given him a bad reference due to jealousy.

OVER SENSITIVE

Whilst the sufferer of NPD is arrogant and haughty, he is also super sensitive to criticism. Pick him up on those little things that are bothering you and you will know about it. Ask him not to call you at work so much as its getting you in trouble with the boss and he will go into a sulk, withdraw and not speak to you. Press him on why he's sulking and you really in for it.

Narcissistic rage is horrific. The first time you experience this it will shock you. This guy who seems to be so in love with you will suddenly turn into a rampaging monster, yelling and calling you horrible names. Eyes wide with anger and a face aggressively contorted beyond recognition from the man who brought you breakfast in bed this morning.

This rage is all your fault. You said something to him that was critical and he wants to make you pay for that. Of course what you said was not what he is now accusing you of saying. In his mind he has distorted it into an ultimate betrayal. Don't ring me so much at work has become "you're a terrible person and I'm ashamed of you". How could you think that about him? All he has done is love you? Do you want him to have a life outside of you? Would you prefer one of those men who don't give their women a second thought all day? Who are out flirting with other women behind your back? Is that what you want, because he can do that, if that's what you want?

Wow! The first time this happens you will back down. You will assume the guilt and apologise profusely. He will eventually calm down, but only after you have admitted you were wrong and a fool and beg him to give you a second chance.

This rage is not even real rage. It is an attempt at control. Basically he is a bully and uses anger to put you back in your cage. The shock you feel at his transformation, the tears you cry as you cower beneath the weight of his anger, are all food to his narcissistic addiction. Look how superior I am to this pathetic creature. I am master of my household!

You dared to criticise him, which made you seem on a level with him, but he can't have that, that doesn't do it for him, so time to slam you down before you get too uppity.

NO APOLOGY

The narc will never apologies. Never. If there is a disagreement, if you get the sulks and the rage, the only way back is for you to accept all responsibility for it, admit you were wrong and apologise to him. Tell him how great he is and how lucky you are to have him in your live. If he still has a use for you he will accept you back. Aren't you grateful for that?

The sulks, silent treatment can go on for ever! It's no detriment to him. He doesn't love you anyway and seeing you suffer because he has withdrawn his attention and affection from you is perfectly natural to him. Whilst you are suffering because you've argued and are not speaking, he is enjoying it! Anyway he knows eventually you will come crawling back and then he can start it all over again. Grand gestures, affirmations of love and devotion, lots of sex. Now you're happy again, you've gotten your fix of his "love" and are his again.

The Narcissist is never wrong. How can he be wrong when he is ultimate perfection?

LACK OF EMPATHY

NPD is a mental illness. It cannot be cured. Some narcissists do learn or are taught to manage it, but the majority of "every day" people have no idea they have this disorder and therefore continue throughout their lives to use people and hurt them for their own gain.

Someone with NPD is unable to feel empathy for other people. For example, if a normal person sees a news report about a lost child, most of us would feel an unbearable pain and sorrow for the parents, imagining how it would feel if it were us. The Narcissist is incapable of feeling this. He would watch the news and then watch The Simpsons and feel exactly the same emotion.

He cannot put himself in other people's shoes. He cannot imagine how it would feel. Why would he? In his world it's all about him and how he is feeling and everyone else on the planet should think the same.

If he is unable to empathise with others, that means he cannot empathise with you. Your pain at his insults and coldness or anger, your frustration and confusion about what the hell did you wrong – none of this affects him on an emotional level. He just does not care.

While a group of us were watching the news about a horrific rape, the Narcissist among us casually remarked that he "felt sorry for the rapist". That is how deranged their thinking is. That is how dangerous they can be.

LIAR

Lying is par for the course. On some level the Narcissist can see that other people behave differently to him. He cannot feel the way they do so, in order to fit, in he will mirror the behaviour he sees in others.

A Narcissistic woman I once knew never kissed or hugged her children until one day she saw a friend hug and kiss her child at the school gate. The woman then began to mirror this action, hugging and kissing her children at the school gate as well. But only at the school gate, where everyone could see what a good mother she was and how her children loved her, once home the children were hardly noticed let alone kissed!

Everything about the Narcissist is a charade. It's a fake profile, a façade put up for a purpose. To gain something. Acceptance into a group, a job, friendship with someone they believe will be useful to them, money and you!

But this false image cannot last. They cannot maintain it. Holes begin to appear. Stories begin to change. Things don't add up or pan out.

For most of us lying is natural. It's a survival instinct. If we get in trouble we will use lying to get out of it. Caught doing something wrong by mum as a child? "I didn't do it...it wasn't me" can save you from punishment. Calling in sick to work to get a duvet day. We also lie to protect others. "No you don't look fat at all" we can reassure a friend so as not to hurt their feelings.

A Narcissist lies as often and as naturally as he breaths. Most everything he says will be a lie. He will twist the truth, leave out important bits, just to sell you on the idea that his fake ID is real and he is the person you want him to be. The façade must be protected at all costs.

Once the lie is found out though, that's when all hell breaks loose.

Chapter 5: Dealing With Pathologically Narcissistic Individuals In Different Settings

Narcissists are interesting as well as engaging individuals but dealing with them daily can be straining as they think that they are the center of the universe and that they have the tendency to look down on others whom they think are below them. When dealing with narcissists, it is important that you tread carefully. They are interesting people but they can lure you into their trap to take advantage over you. Below are tips that will help you deal with people who are pathologically narcissists.

Determine If You Are Dealing With A Narcissist or Not

It is important that you know the difference between persons who are suffering from narcissistic personality disorder from someone who has a very strong self-image. Remember that all people have tendencies to become narcissists but not everyone suffers from this disorder. A pathological narcissist puts themselves first and they are always aware of how important they are. Unfortunately, they don't care about other people whom they think are below them thus they put other people down and have a tendency to bully them. On the other hand, people with strong self-image only make a strong projection of themselves and they do not bully other people in order to attract attraction.

Don't Let Yourself Get Sucked Up Into Their Plan

Narcissists will only approach you if they have plans to gain something from you. You have to take note that narcissists have the tendency to see people as objects for their own entertainment. They can easily pull your strings and make you do whatever it is that they want you to do. When you deal with a narcissist, make sure that you do not let yourself get sucked by their plans.

Always Keep Your Distance

Narcissists are very cunning especially if they want to get something from you. They are very charming and deceiving and their charm can often cause people to question their concerns. If you believe that you are dealing with a pathological narcissist, make sure that you keep your distance.

Guard Your Mind and Heart

Make sure that you guard both your heart and mind. Although it is difficult to neither reach out to people nor get involved with a person suffering from narcissistic personality disorder, you have to remember that narcissists will also never let you into their lives. It might sound very cold but it is the only way to protect yourself from being used by a narcissist.

Always Review Your Decision to Help a Narcissist

Most pathological narcissists are keen on asking many favors from people around them. If you want to help a narcissist, then you should review your decision to do something for them as they can see this as an opportunity to use you. If, however, you really want to help a narcissist out, make sure that you hold your ground. If you the things that you are doing for the sake of a narcissist are making you uncomfortable, then probably it is not doing you good anymore. Stop what you are doing and firmly decline the narcissist that you are no longer willing to do the things that he or she asks of you.

Treat Them Neutrally

Remember that people who suffer from narcissistic personality disorder want to be the center of the attention. If you don't want to be used by a narcissist, treat them neutrally and equally as you would other people.

Keep Realistic Expectations

Narcissistic people have endearing qualities but their limited emotional maturity makes it difficult to deal with them. Thus, it is important you accept the fact and keep realistic expectations that they have a lot of limitations when it comes to connecting with you.

Don't Depend On Them

The problem with some people is that they get engrossed with their beguiling charm. As such, most people end up being emotionally dependent on them by confiding their deepest feelings as well as secrets to a narcissistic individual.

Show How Things Can Be To Their Benefit

Remember that people who suffer from narcissistic personality disorder are those who only look at things that will benefit them. In order to communicate with them successfully, show them how things can be to their benefit. If you want to motivate a narcissist, tell them how they can benefit from the task to boost their ego. For instance, instead of telling your narcissistic partner "I really would appreciate it if you go with me to the family reunion", you can say "Everyone likes you so will you accompany me to the family reunion?"

Narcissists are rapidly proliferating in different settings everywhere. This means that you are certain to encounter narcissists wherever you may go at any time and day. While the tips mentioned above are general strategies to deal with narcissists, it is important that you know how to deal with them at specific environments. In the succeeding sections, a discussion on how you can deal with narcissists in different conditions will be discussed.

Chapter 6: The Impact Of Fear And Anger

As mentioned in Chapter 1, Narcissists do not cope well with emotions. Fear and anger are among the two most powerful human emotions, and they are the two most troublesome to Narcissists. There are several different reasons that this is the case.

First, fear and anger are emotions. Emotions are individualized and specific to the person experiencing them. Every individual will react to these emotions in his or her own specific way. Some people are excellent at managing one or both of these emotions, but most people will admit that one or both causes them extreme discomfort. They might also add that their actions and reactions in response to fear and anger leave them feeling bad for some period of time.

You need to consider how well you deal with fear and anger, and ask yourself if your fears are real and do you really have good cause to be angry?

A Narcissist will find a way to transfer or assign blame to someone or something when they feel these emotions, at least in most cases.

When something goes wrong for them, they will find a way of blaming someone else, as they generally consider that they do not make mistakes. For instance, simple things like overfilling a box that then breaks under the weight will be because they have been given an inferior box, not because of their misjudgment in the strength of the box. They will be very angry with whoever gave them the box, blaming them for the disaster.

But this is just an example, whatever goes wrong for them, they will always find someone else to blame. They will be angry with that person often resorting to insults as a way of trying to belittle the person in retaliation for causing the Narcissist a problem.

Outbursts of this nature only make relationships even harder for them to maintain, but they fail to see how they are hurting the feelings of other people and how they are driving friends and relations away from them.

You probably recognize this type of behavior in others when it happens, thinking to yourself that they are over-reacting.

There will always be times when we have an angry reaction that is not warranted. If you are going through a stressful period in your life, behaving in this way becomes more usual, but for the Narcissist, it becomes part of their normal behavior, and they can see nothing wrong with it. They see shouting at people as their right, sometimes feeling that this is the only way anyone listens to them. This feeling just compounds the disorder, as if they begin to find that being angry gets the results they want, the more often they will knowingly use this to gain their own desires.

But this is not true anger, more of a show of anger without the feelings inside, as real anger is an emotion a Narcissist has problems dealing with.

Very often, there is no real justification for the outburst, and someone without NPD would not act in this way, but neither would they be attention seeking as an NPD sufferer does.

Narcissism is often a cycle of fear and anger for the sufferer. The affected individual fears that no one is listening to his concerns, feelings, and intelligence. When the conversation leans toward what someone else cares about or thinks, the Narcissist becomes angry, and often ends the conversation abruptly or has an outburst – in order to get more attention and because of the need to be recognized as valued.

What about fear? Fear is a strong motivating force for anyone. We have all heard the term, fight or flight. These are the two reactions that human beings and animals have to fear. If you fear something, it is human nature to try and avoid it. If you can't avoid it, you fight against it. A Narcissist will often fear conversation and confrontation, because he or she is worried that his or her opinions and feelings won't be considered.

Of course, we know that the Narcissist will be considering only his or her agenda during the course of the conversation –

but what happens when the other person isn't thinking about the same?

Fear and anger are the Narcissist's biggest enemies, two that cannot easily be tamed. It is possible for someone with Narcissistic tendencies to break the cycle of fear and anger, but it takes a significant amount of thought and introspection to conquer the hold that emotion will oftentimes have over an individual. It is in beating these two emotions that therapy can sometimes be the most help.

Chapter 7: What Makes Narcissists Tick

Narcissists often lack a mature conscience. The one thing they fear is being punished or suffering any form of damage to their reputations. Yes, they are often religious and pessimistic as all get-out.

Like the Narcissus of old, Narcissists are often so invested in appearances; theirs and others and the truth is that they would often lie to keep up appearances. A Narcissist would sooner tell you he works in the White House than admit he has been out of a job for a good while.

They love to hear themselves talk and they are terrible listeners; in fact when you start speaking they often tune out or glaze over, unless of course you are talking about them. They can't understand that you would have anything more important to do than drop everything you are doing and listen to them all the time. They love to be praised and praised and praised.

Narcissists adapt to their environment so don't expect to be able to spot one right off, every time. Don't expect say the narcissist local farmer to be as obvious as the narcissist senior lawyer. Besides, some narcissists are super-religious and supposedly pious thus prompting them to hide that part of themselves and act all nice until Mr. Jekyll shows his hairy face.

Narcissists can affect different personalities when in the stores, the church, the office, and at home; radically different personalities.

Narcissists rarely look within, they are more impressed by the exterior and perhaps it is this inherent inability or unwillingness to engage in self-examination of any form that has made them so hard to pull out of their disorder.

71

Narcissists often have an excess of energy; they are usually highly motivated, assertive and yep, competitive. The tendency to be bullies is very high in narcissistic personalities and you have to develop a backbone and stand up for yourself or else they would toss you about as mercilessly as possible. Often it isn't even deliberate because they really don't stop to think about it. It just comes automatically and in the fall-out, you get the worst end of it.

Narcissists are more often a product of nurture than of nurture. No, this is not the part where you point your fingers at the parents and say narcissism is their fault. Narcissism is a product of environment, events and more importantly choice. People **choose** to adopt certain habits and those habits soon form part of their personalities.

Narcissists are extremely sensitive to personal criticism and conversely critical of other people; it's just one of the weird wirings in their makeup.

Chapter 8: Narcissistic Personality Disorder

As discussed, we all have a little narcissism in us, and many people manage everyday life successfully, despite the condition. However, when taken to its extreme, narcissism becomes Narcissistic Personality Disorder. This is a disorder where the individual has an extremely inflated sense of their own importance and a deep desire for admiration and adoration. They are preoccupied with power and prestige to an extreme degree, and are unable to see the damage this is doing to their own lives, and to the lives of others they interact and are involved with.

People with Narcissistic Personality Disorder (NPD) are often described as self centered, cocky, demanding, and manipulative. Someone with NPD will likely be convinced that they deserve special treatment, and will act like it too. They will also likely engage in aggressive behavior, and risk-taking activities. Symptoms of NPD include:

- Reacting to criticism with anger or humiliation
- Taking advantage of others to reach their own goal
- Exaggeration of their own importance, talents and/or achievements
- Entertains unrealistic fantasies about gaining success, power, intelligence or romantic relationships
- Has an expectation of favorable treatment
- Expect others to simply go along with any of their ideas and plans
- Expressing dislike or disdain for those they find inferior to themselves
- Requires constant attention and adoration from others
- Becomes jealous easily, and believes that others are always jealous of themselves

•Pays little attention to the feelings of others, and pursues selfish goals
•While coming across as very tough-minded, can in fact be hurt easily

There are different theories on the causes of narcissism. Although most believe that genes play a heavy involvement, opinions differ on the environmental causes. Some believe that narcissism stems from neglect or abuse very early in life, while others believe that in fact the opposite, over-indulgence and unabated praise, with few limits set by parents, is the more likely cause. Another school of thought is that narcissism itself does not develop until the teen years. Some think that narcissism peeks as teens, and mellows by middle age, while others still profess that narcissism will only get worse with age, as their grandiose plans fail to come to fruition and their physical attributes lessen as they naturally age.

Whatever the cause, narcissists live in a world where they cannot trust the outside environment and other people to meet their emotional needs. In their own minds, they are complete unto themselves, with no need for anything that someone else can give them.

Many confuse narcissism with very high self esteem, but there is an important and clear difference. NPD crosses over from healthy self esteem into self adoration. A narcissist puts themselves on a pedestal, and expects others will naturally recognize their brilliance. Someone with a healthy high self esteem, while they will love themselves, does not value themselves as more important than other people or above others in their life.

Narcissists have an inherit belief that they are due special treatment simply for who they are, and can become very angry, very quickly, when they are denied it. Often the other person will have no idea that how they acted has been perceived as a slight towards the narcissist.

When this happens, something called narcissistic rage can occur swiftly. The term was first used in 1972, by Heinz Kohut, and Austrian born American psychoanalyst who studied narcissism extensively. It was Sigmund Freud who first realized that narcissists felt an implied injury in the 1920's, and Kohut has expanded further on this condition.

Kohut believed that because of how a narcissist views their sense of self, their very self is being called into question with the perceived narcissistic injury. They are therefore prone to oversensitivity to any perceived slight towards themselves, resulting in narcissistic rage. They must react strongly so as to regain total control over their environment. They must both remove the other person's ability to harm them, while regaining control over the situation and rebuilding their inflated sense of self, to restore their own sense of safety and power. The narcissist may also feel a strong sense of shame over their 'failures' being called into the open, which may also result in the stronger reactions of narcissistic rage.

A perceived insult or threat towards the narcissist can lead them to feel extremely targeted or injured. When these symptoms of anger are expressed in return, they are called a narcissistic rage. Symptoms can range from relatively mild and non-violet, to an extreme outburst. They may range from simply ignoring the perceived injurer, or being mildly annoyed, through to full on, violent attacks.

More subtle reactions may also include the narcissist being visibly irritated, 'tisking' or shaking their head, or expressing vocal disagreement with the situation. A more severe rage can include outbursts of physical violence, both at objects and people, shouting and strong physical actions. You may have seen athletes who throw the bat across the field when they are called out, or know someone labeled a 'sore loser' – these are both examples of narcissist rage.

What's important to recognize with narcissistic rage is that it differs from true anger in that it is unwarranted, and often caused by a neutral event that a non-narcissist would struggle to even identify. Real anger is a natural response to an identified frustrating or annoying event, and will usually dissipate after the anger expressed. In opposition, a narcissist rage can blow significantly out of proportion, and continue well after the initial event. Some narcissists find themselves trapped in a cycle or rage that perpetuates itself, while others may only experience the occasional burst when in a perceived extreme scenario. It is also not unlikely to find the sudden burst of rage to be followed swiftly by the 'silent treatment', both of which are used as a method to punish the perceived offender.

If you find yourself faced with narcissistic rage, the first thing to remember is to not engage. You will never be able to 'win' the argument, or make the narcissist believe that you did not mean to offend them. If you react in any way, it will only serve to exacerbate their anger. Almost any response you give, sans agreeing with the narcissist, will fan the flames and could escalate the situation to physical violence. Even logic and reason will not help once the situation has escalated to this level, and nothing that you say or do can change the narcissist's beliefs at that moment.

If faced with a narcissistic rage, the best thing you can do is walk away and refuse to engage with that person, even at a later time. If you are unable to do this, there are several methods you can use to limit your risk and exposure.

First, establish your personal boundaries, how much you are willing to put up with. If you reach this threshold, then leave the room, or the house. They may follow you, but if you do this consistently, the narcissist will learn that you will not react to their rage attacks.

Learn how to keep yourself calm. If you cannot remove yourself from the situation, then showing no reaction at all is also beneficial. Learn how to calm your breathing and anxiety and try to create a sense of detachment from the behavior. If you continually show no recognition or reaction to their anger, it will give you some control of the situation.

Following that, simply accept their point of view, just for that moment. Remember, that the rage is not about you, or anything real that you did. Whatever you say to justify your behavior will not be heard at this moment. Once the narcissistic person has calmed down at a later time, you can try to discuss the issues that lead you to the reaction in the first place.

So, what hope exists for both those diagnosed with NPD, and their loved ones? Although at first, narcissists may come across as very popular and charming, the long term social outcomes for those with NPD are not good. Long term relationships are difficult, as people become wise to their true natures, and on average, general levels of narcissism drop dramatically by age 30 across the general population. When this happens, such behavior is deemed more and more unacceptable by their peers. If the narcissist continues as they grow older, they can find themselves ignored completely by their peers.

But, is it even possible for anyone to change their very personality? The cause of NPD is not widely agreed or understood. Like many personality disorders, the cause is thought to be a combination of genetics and environment. It's believed that genes may play a significant role, up to 50%. But, along with this, the unique experience of each person and their interactions with others influences whether an individual will develop narcissism, and to what degree. This includes a relatively new influx of cultural factors that encourage narcissism.

It's thought that individuals with NPD come from a background where being vulnerable was treated badly, or was seen as a defect. They fear being dependant on anyone else, for any reason. People affected with NPD have learnt to suppress and ignore any perceived incompetency or vulnerability and hide it under a mask of self importance and competence. It's not that people with this personality disorder cannot change at all, but that doing so threatens their very self, the image that they are perfect and can do no wrong. This lack of flexibility or willingness to change then creates failed relationships, which simply reinforces their original position.

To explain, you cannot be narcissistic alone. You need the adoration of fans and reinforcement of your superiority. As time goes on however, they have a moment of narcissistic rage, or they let something show they didn't meant to let slip, and the fear that they will be 'found out' grows, and you show less and less of your true self. The very same people the narcissist was trying to impress become alienated, and this convinces the person with NPD that they need to do better to hide their flaws next time, and so the cycle goes on.

Even if they should meet someone who seems to see beyond their mask, and could offer a more authentic relationship, most sufferers of NPD are convinced that this only means they will somehow eventually be deemed unworthy. This fear builds up, and unfortunately, this means that those closest to the narcissist will often be the ones who suffer the most projected anger and rages. The greatest irony of the condition is that the efforts narcissists put in place to protect their sense of self, are in the end the cause of the rejection that they fear so much.

The first stage of treating NPD then can become an effort to change the traditional relationship patterns that a narcissistic person relies on. To encourage them that they can be loved, warts and all, if they will let someone in. The wall of protection can then soften and eventually possibly give way to true intimacy and emotion. There is no cure for Narcissistic Personality Disorder, but with psychotherapy people can learn to relate and react to others in a more positive way. The goal of psychotherapy is to help the narcissistic person to develop better true self esteem and also more realistic expectations of others around them. If the case is severe, then medication may also treat the more serious symptoms.

Clinical diagnosis and treatment for NPD can be rare however, due to the narcissist's close held belief that they are something special, and the mere suggestion that there could be something with them that needs addressing can send them into a downward spiral. Information however shows that narcissists can learn to be more caring about others, which in turn reduces their own narcissistic tendencies as they participate in more social interactions.

However, new research from Wilfrid Laurier University has suggested that narcissism may be less complex that previous research suggests. The study suggests that rather than being a complex moral failing, narcissism may be simply a mechanical failure of the brain to mimic, something that comes so easily to most of us that we do not realize what we're doing.

Humans regularly use mimicry to inadvertently copy others in a social situation, for example taking a sip of your own drink when a person sitting opposite you does so. Professor Sukhvinder Obhi, who undertook the research, states that he believes that rather than this being innate, the ability to mimic is learned on an individual basis. He believes that this ability is what starts the bridge towards empathy and true understanding of others.

For a narcissist, who has not developed this ability, their understanding of appreciating what others are thinking is hampered by their lack of understanding and mirroring of others actions. The narcissist therefore takes a more basic, utilitarian view of others. They believe that narcissists do not mirror other's behavior and actions naturally, and this leads to them having real problems fitting in with social situations. By training this behavior, he believes that narcissism could be lessened.

Chapter 9: Stages Of Narcissist Grief

In the standardized grief process, there are five stages of grief, which are denial, anger, bargaining, depression, and acceptance. When it comes to grieving the loss after narcissistic abuse, there are seven. I have listed the stages below, and they are not necessarily in any order. One stage can last for days, two weeks to months, years; there is no set time. Grieving is a process, be patient with yourself as you embrace the grief. It's very common to go back and forth into different stages of grief.

The seven stages of grief from a narcissistic, abusive relationship are:

1. Absolute Devastation: This is the initial stage, where we realize we have been a victim of this type of sickening abuse. We are shocked to our core. We realize our loved one(s), never truly loved us as they were incapable of it,

they used, exploited and deliberately chose us to try to destroy us emotionally, financially, etc. We were abused and used horrendously. This first realization of the truth is both shocking and devastating. It's as if a light switch went on in our brain and we have a new understanding that it wasn't our fault and that we have been victimized. The truth and reality of the situation has hit. This is actually life-saving as we know the truth and it's the truth we have been seeking. Everything now makes sense, it clicks, and we now get it. This truth even though is enlightening, it is also absolutely devastating and debilitating. We can also be devastated as we may learn some of our friendships we have had for years, may also be narcissistic. There may be a double loss or more involved.

2. Denial and Self-Doubt. We may re-hash our coming out of the fog moment, and now we question it. We re-evaluate our new truth and deny it. We think we have made a grave error. In this phase, we doubt, question and deny the realization of the truth.

3. Education. Once we have come to terms with the reality and we agree we have been victimized, education is key to learn about the situation. We research and learn about narcissism. We desire to know the truth and for it all to make sense. At this stage, we may have more questions than answers.

4. Anger: Not only are we angry at our wronged circumstance and have to face the consequences and fallout that has occurred; we are furious at the situation we find ourselves in. Our lives have changed, we are faced with

having to make new life-altering decisions. We are in a mess; it has hit home.

5. Depression. Activities once enjoyed, may be of absolutely no interest. We want to sleep and recover. In this sage, we find we may not have the emotional strength to do the things once loved. Our body and mind is grieving and needs time to recover.

6. Healing and validation. We have come to understand that we have been a victim of narcissistic abuse, are now see ourselves as a survivor. Coming this far is a huge victory and has been worth the effort we have put in. Hard work has been done, and the ability to talk about the situation with desiring revenge has been accomplished.

7. Self-Discovery. This is the part of the healing and grieving process where we look introspectively at ourselves. We have a desire to learn why this abuse

has occurred. We look to see what characteristics or qualities or lack in our lives has led us to this situation. We take responsibility and look to see how we can change and better ourselves and to prevent this from occurring again. This is a journey of knowing our needs, engaging in self-loving behaviors, and being able to communicate and establish healthy boundaries with others effectively.

There are tough stages in the grieving process. Some stages possess unique challenges to us since the narcissist has brainwashed us to believe in a different reality. They have created an atmosphere where we doubt our self, situations, and we may become confused with our own reality. It's like waking up from the matrix. What we were told is not true. What we believed never happened. What we thought never occurred.

Get rest, sleep, and set time aside to allow time to recover. Set time to relax. It's okay not to be a social butterfly and hop around town going to events. Mourn. Grieve. Cancel appointments. Get in touch with what happened. Learn. See a therapist or a counselor who is specialized with narcissist abuse trauma. Realize you have been through an emotional hell, with adrenaline working overtime, body in flight-or-fight for a long time. It's time to get rest in all forms and recover. There is light at the end of the tunnel. It will get better.

Losing Friends and/or Family

There can be a heavy loss involved as one recover from narcissistic abuse. There can be a loss of friends and family, loss of a spouse, and spouse's family. As we reach out to discuss this with friends, we may get odd looks. They may not understand what has happened and will not be able to assist with recovery. We seek to be understood and validated by our friends and close loved ones. As disheartening as it may be, even our friends who we have had for years that we have allowed into our lives may also carry unhealthy traits of narcissism which we never saw before. The impact of this dual discovery can also be devastating. A counselor or therapist who specialized in narcissistic abuse will be a great resource and safe avenue to aid in the recovery and healing process.

Chapter 10: Where Does This Attitude Problem Come From?

Many children are simply born with a melancholy personality or melancholy temperament. The narcissist might have been a grumpy baby who came out of the womb chronically unhappy with himself and his life. The narcissist may have autism, learning deficits, ADHD, sensory processing disorder and asperger's syndrome or schizoid personality disorder that make navigating the world difficult. He may have had head injuries in childhood or infancy, may have had oxygen deprivation which caused him brain damage, or may have had an illness which caused brain damage.

Some children have syndromes which are genetically passed down from the parents to their children. They may have had illnesses, allergies, physical disabilities or awkwardness that impeded their ability to socialize and play with other children in healthy ways. Children who are not appropriately socialized and who do not learn social skills early on often have difficulty reading the intentions of others later in life. This can lead to bullying and rejection by one's peers.

Boys often seem to have more difficulties with social skills and emotional maturity than girls do. Boys are also taught by their parents, teachers and other adults not to cry and to cover up their feelings. This leaves men and boys clamming up about things that they should be talking to their peers and support system about. They can feel lonely rather than getting guidance from someone else. They can feel that their feelings are 'wrong', or that they don't fit in with others because they have feelings that they don't see as appropriate.

People with narcissistic traits might have been subjected to trauma in life. They may have lost someone in their life that they were close to, may have fallen ill with an inexplicable or incurable disorder, may have learning or attention deficits, may have dyslexia or auditory processing disorder which causes them an inability to hear others correctly or to follow directions, or may have other syndromes or disorders. Most of these disorders are never diagnosed.

Many families with health problems and mental problems that run genetically in the family never have good enough jobs or insurance to properly diagnose every disorder that a child has. Some children are born into families where domestic violence or codependency issues in the relationships of the parents cause issues so that the children are largely neglected while they are growing up. The children might be victims of divorce, suicide, homicide, infidelity, alcoholism, drug problems and more. A child may grow up in a family where they were not planned, were not wanted, and where they caused significant burden to the parents involved. A child may have witnessed a trauma at school, may have been sexually abused by adults in their lives, or may have been the victim of incest in the family. A child may be a latchkey kid as a result of parents who have to work too much in order to afford necessities of daily life. Or a child may not see any emotional intimacy or affection being shared by their parents.

There are other causes of negativistic thinking and a negativistic outlook on life. A child could be extremely gifted, talented and intelligent, but may be born to parents of average or below-average intelligence. This child may suffer feelings that he or she does not belong or does not fit in with his family long into adulthood.

A child with a high IQ may struggle to find conversations with lower IQ children or adults uninteresting. He may fail to engage with his parents or peers, or he may feel that his parents never attune to him due to the IQ difference between himself and others.

Negativistic children may grow up around hoards or negativistic, pessimistic and petty adults. The adults may chronically complain about their life and their unhappiness, leading the child to believe that life is all about unhappiness and chronic disdain for others. A child might believe that chronic complaining and cursing are the only acceptable form of conversation and communication if he is only around adults who are negativistic and sarcastic.

The negativistic and temperamental child may immerse himself only in crude humor and violence at the expense of others because his friends or family feel this is acceptable behavior. He may only immerse himself in disgusting or inappropriate movies or adult films which are acceptable by his immediate peers, so that he is accepted for telling distasteful jokes.

The negativistic and temperamental child may learn from inappropriate adults that being inappropriate equates to being a 'man'. He might learn that hitting, abuse, criticism and disdain toward women is healthy and appropriate. He might learn that he must 'put a woman in her place' the way that his grandfather and great-grandfather may have done during the years of the depression. He fails to realize that there was a feminine movement, that women now have choices, and that they might not choose a negativistic and pessimistic man who feels it is quite acceptable to bully women.

The negativistic and temperamental child may be slave to his own bodily functions, his sensitivities, his allergies, his awkward body movements, and his body dysmorphic disorder. Someone may have laughed at him, made fun of his body, made him feel 'fat' or 'out of shape, or he may have come up with this conclusion on his own. He cannot accept himself for who he is. He was made to feel that every human must be perfect.

The narcissist cannot tolerate his own imperfections, thus he ignores them or projects them onto others. He cannot tolerate his own social deficits, and thus socially acceptable small talk with others is seen as pointless, a nuisance to him. He hates having to turn off his autopilot, to think of things to say, and hates wondering why people look at him strangely when he says something that is socially inappropriate. He sulks and whines that other people 'don't get him', that they don't understand his bland humor, and that he doesn't actively listen in order to learn anything at all about the other person's likes and dislikes.

The narcissist cannot attend to even a minor conversation with his mouth shut and his ears open. He is ready to defend his opinion, jump on his soapbox, fill your head with nonsensical information that some adult taught him long ago that has long since gone out of fashion. His mind is filled with old knowledge, incomplete knowledge and outdated information, because his learning deficits make it extremely difficult for him to learn something new that is outside of his comfort zone.

All of these things make the narcissist chronically dissatisfied, insanely unhappy, and antisocial. Occasionally, the narcissist can put on a fake face to draw in some unsuspecting victim into his negativistic layer. He will criticize this person to death until they leave him or kill themselves because he has made them equally depressed and unresponsive to life. The narcissist will never kill himself, however. He sees no reason to do so, even in his pits of misery and despair. He isn't emotional or empathetic, and thus his logical and analytical brain sees no point to ending his life early even when he is making others around him want to end their own just by simply being associated with this emotional vampire.

Chapter 11: Further Understanding The Narcissist

Narcissistic people are difficult to deal with, because they only care about what's on the outside, and they like to feign invulnerability. This is one of the areas where the arrogant and narcissistic personalities differ greatly. It has already been established that narcissists are perfectionists, so showing the slightest amount of pain is something they rarely do. Admitting pain is equal to admitting they have a weakness, so the narcissist will try to hurt you instead of try to work out the issue. This is especially true if you're the one who cased the pain. On the other hand, arrogant people will complain about the most minor of details. Unfortunately, the narcissistic are also typically very vengeful. They express hurt feelings by hurting the feelings of others. These individuals are known for their competitive nature, which even manifests itself in their relationships. Everything is a competition and they're determined to win, even if you're not aware that you're competing.

Preparing For Battle

There's an undeniable relationship with vengeance and narcissism. It has been well detailed by some of the world's foremost psychological experts, including Sigmund Freud. There are a number of reasons leading to the vengeance but the cocky attitude is a big part of it. They can't believe that you would have the audacity to do or say something of which they didn't approve. It's important to remember that the narcissist sees him or herself as being much better than other people, which usually also includes the other person in the relationship. Since your significant other feels you're inferior, it causes more rage when you do something wrong.

It's like an ant insulting a God, even if you didn't intend to seem audacious. Worst of all, you don't really have to do anything wrong to provoke the wrath of a narcissist. These individuals live in worlds where the perspectives of others are irrelevant. Even reality doesn't matter to a narcissist, because he or she feels immune to the rules of society and even physics.

Even events that are beyond your control can upset the narcissist. If you got invited to a special event but you experienced car trouble, most people would simply dismiss it as bad fortune. However, the narcissist will be angry that you didn't foresee the car trouble. You'll be ridiculed for not keeping the car properly tuned because the narcissist doesn't think the misfortune could have befallen him or her. Even asking what you should have done differently won't prevent the narcissist from getting upset.

Fighting For The Sake Of Fighting

With a narcissist, it's not about working out the issue; it's about winning the battle of hurting your feelings. These individuals are typically very impulsive and they'll permanently damage a long-term relationship on a whim. To the narcissist you intentionally experienced car trouble in an effort to cause strife. It's important to remember that narcissists live in worlds where reality doesn't exist. They put total faith into what they believe and anyone who disagrees is wrong. Once these people have been hurt, they will seek to hurt you as well. Revenge can be something as simple as spitting in your food while you're not looking, but it really depends upon how hurt the other person feels. This is the difficult thing about being in a relationship with someone who's narcissistic. It's important to remember that these people feel like they're perfect and they'll expect the same from you.

Narcissistic people are very successful because they can't accept anything less than the absolute best. They think of themselves as being able to conquer the world, and they can only learn things the hard way. They'll enter situations where they face insurmountable odds, because they think they can still win. Since they believe themselves to be flawless, they expect the same from you. Anytime you disappoint a narcissistic person, you can expect swift and substantial retaliation.

It may be something as small as a few insults for not being so perfect, but the other person will never say, "You hurt me". Anytime he or she feels hurt, it becomes a race to hurt you back – and it will be a competition. If you slightly embarrass your significant other, he or she will embarrass you a lot. Your intentions are irrelevant,   because narcissists think they know why you did whatever it was that has upset them. If you spill something on the narcissistic person by accident, he or she might throw wine on you intentionally.

If you kiss someone else the narcissistic person may sleep with your sibling or even your aunt or uncle. These types of people regularly work out and eat healthy so they're very physically attractive. It won't be difficult to find someone close to you with whom they can have an affair. Worst of all, there will be no effort made to hide the indiscretion as the unfaithful party will broadcast the deed in an effort to hurt you more. It's a dirty game that nobody can win, but the abuse brings the narcissistic person momentary joy.

Other people will think there must have been something else that triggered such irresponsible behavior, but it really doesn't take much. This is multiplied by the fact that they internalize their emotional pain, for months on end. This makes them increasingly frustrated and volatile, and they'll try to go to extreme lengths to convince the world that there's nothing wrong. Holding onto the pain for so long is a contributor to their volatility, because it can erupt forward without any agitation. According to some psychologists, internalizing emotions can be dangerous of even fatal. However, narcissists vent their emotions, but usually at the wrong time.

Bad Temper, Bad Decision

Narcissists are masters of timing which is how they become so successful. Remember that they're inflated ego is well deserved, because they have accomplished great things in life. However, they've done this by defying odds that other people would have never dared to face. Therefore, they will wait until the moment is right to get back at you. It can be like waiting for the other shoe to drop, because there will certainly be revenge. These individuals have convinced themselves that they are invincible, but of course the people they love have the ability to hurt them. Unfortunately, narcissists convince themselves that their pain is actually anger, and they treat it that way. This is the way that they have achieved in life, because they use disappointment, frustration, anger, despair and every other emotion as fuel for their success. Pain motivates them to take action, even if you didn't mean to cause them any pain at all. It's all about meeting their expectations, but this is a nearly impossible task.

Appreciate The Narcissism

Unlike an arrogant person with false confidence, the narcissist can't simply be broken down with inconvenient truths. With the arrogant person, it's easy to point out how proud he or she is about a nominal accomplishment. However, pointing out the accomplishments of the narcissists will only strengthen his or her confidence. It's also a very bad idea to try to get the narcissist to make epic changes. This person has unbelievable drive which is probably depended upon by many other people. Narcissists may be taking care of their retired parents or other people who are struggling. If you do manage to convince your partner to change, he or she may become far less profitable. Your entire way of life is probably dependent upon the narcissism, and your partner will be a completely different person without it. The six pack abs become a beer belly, you have traded the Mercedes for a Toyota and sell the house to get an apartment. Most self-made millionaires are extremely narcissistic. Most of these millionaires also went bankrupt at least three times before getting rich. In short, true narcissism is actually a good trait in some ways. This individual could lose everything tomorrow and he or she would have it back within a matter of years.

Meeting Their Life Expectancies

Dean Koontz is an extremely successful suspense author and he's probably a diehard narcissist. Dean Koontz isn't even his real name, but that's irrelevant. Mr. Koontz wrote a novel titled Life Expectancy. In the book, Dean explains that the term life expectancy refers to what a person actually expects from life. Narcissists are successful, because they have ridiculous life expectancies. A narcissist will take a job in the mail room with expectations of becoming the CEO. He or she will even have a detailed plan to help accomplish this lofty goal. When you met this individual, you realized that something was very different. Narcissists have personalities that draw others in, and they love the attention. They also strive for the very best of everything, because they hate to settle. This also applies to the relationship which is why it's so hard to stay with a narcissist.

the amount of compliments they give you, it's probably for a reason. Trust your intuition and feelings.

Chapter 12: Healthy Narcissism

You can't begin to understand the personality disorder classified as NPD without investigating current thinking on so called "healthy narcissism". Everyone needs to feel good about themselves and pursue a life of achievement and success. It is very difficult, especially in our free market, competitive economy, to thrive in life if one carries the baggage of a negative self-image and goes through life without any self-confidence. This idea of healthy narcissism comes from a theory in psychology called object relations.

We All Are Objects In Someone's Subconscious

The idea is that adults will relate to others based on their experience as infants relating to their parents. Images of how they were treated as infants become "objects" in their subconscious. As adults, when other people remind them of their parents, the subconscious will predict how this person is going to behave toward them. If the object in their subconscious mind produces memories of mistreatment or neglect, or memories of happiness and nurturing, the behavior predicted by the subconscious will correspond to the memory. Thus the idea that people are treated as objects because of the objects that "live" in the subconscious formed in infancy and early childhood was "born" with this theory. The process of predicting at the subconscious level how someone is going to be treated by another has a tremendous effect on a person's family and social relationships.

A Healthy Relationship With Subconscious Objects And Therefore With Others In Life A healthy narcissist will have subconscious objects that facilitate the proper behavior toward others they have relationships with, giving the healthy narcissist the ability to both receive and give gratifying engagements and have gratifying experiences with others in their life. Healthy subconscious objects help to build a truthful self-image that is in balance with the ego and there is no need to treat people as objects to be used solely for the purpose of achievement and self-aggrandizement.

The Causes Of Pathological Narcissism
It is reported that narcissism becomes unhealthy and pathological when one cannot love the objects stored in their subconscious and the frustration this creates produces an obsession with self-love and the megalomania behavior that follows.

Chapter 13: Dealing With Narcissism And Npd

At this point, you have to accept that dealing with narcissism and NPD is a challenge. Whether you have NPD or you're dealing with someone who has one, it's still going to be hard and you're going to need a lot of patience. The first step in solving any problem is admitting there is one and it's no different with NPD. Coping with the disorder is hard but it possible if you know what to do.

Coping with NPD

The most stressful thing about having NPD is seeing how other people react around you. Friends, family, or acquaintances may not want to be around you, making social interaction a painful experience for anyone with NPD. But how do you cope with something that you don't even feel consciously?

Don't Blame Yourself

The first thing you have to do is stop blaming yourself. You have to accept that NPD is a medical condition and it wasn't your fault that it developed. You didn't do anything to have this sort of behavior and accepting that will let you open up and trust people more and start working your way in dealing with the narcissistic tendencies that you have.

Asking Help from Your Family

The most available support system is the family and that goes for those with NPD. The great thing about family as a support system is because of their availability and acceptance. Having people accept you for who you are and regardless of how you act is something that narcissists cherish the most, especially when they recognize that they have a behavioral problem. Asking help from your own family is one of the best things that you can do and is the first essential step in seeking treatment for NPD.

Venting Out and Sharing Emotions

Most narcissists have this problem in sharing emotions because they perceive venting out and sharing emotions as a form of weakness. You have to understand that even though emotions may be a sign of weakness for you, it becomes an open avenue for understanding for the people around you. There's no harm in venting out emotions from time to time and as long as it's through a healthy channel, then venting out will be a positive experience that will let you explore your feelings and understand yourself more.

Setting Ground Rules

One part of behavioral therapy for NPD is setting rules to follow. If you're determined to resolve your behavior and fight off narcissistic tendencies, setting ground rules and sticking to them is important. This way, you get to limit yourself and provide a sense of control over your behaviors. Gaining back control and seeing it through will give you an incredible feeling of accomplishment that will boost your self-esteem in the most rational and believable way wherein you won't need to get self-centered and realize that you do have what it takes to be humble and down to earth.

Understanding the Past of Someone with NPD

There are several factors that may lead to the development of NPD and you are no exception. Blaming yourself again and again isn't going to help either. Exploring your past and recognizing events that may have triggered your NPD is a key factor in treatment and moving forward. It may stem from factors like child abuse, bullying, abusive parents, a traumatic incident from school or work, or more. Knowing these factors that may have happened in the past and addressing them accordingly

Setting Goals

In order to set things right and steady, you need to set some goals for yourself to reach. Setting goals is a therapeutic approach in behavioral therapy as it allows you to have direction and purpose during the course of treatment. While those with NPD may show great signs for being leaders and workers, their skewed views of themselves and their abilities may hinder them from accomplishing the tasks. It's important to set attainable goals—this plants a narcissist's feet down to the ground and realize his or her limitations.

Interacting with a Narcissist

It's hard to interact with a narcissist, no matter who you are. Friends, family, or colleagues at work have trouble in dealing with narcissists. In NPD, these narcissistic tendencies are natural to them and reacting in a negative way won't help solve the problem, in fact, that will just make it even worse. So how do you interact with a narcissist?

Talking to Someone with NPD

Initiating a conversation with someone who has NPD is difficult. Their personality may come as arrogant or haughty, inciting a condescending reaction from you, but it's important that you hold back on your own emotions if you want to have a proper conversation with someone who has NPD. First, you have to approach with a gentleness and care if you want to preserve your relationship with a narcissist. Don't immediately point out mistakes or criticize them for their behavior as this will damage their built up self-image and confidence. Say what you want in a calm and respectful manner. If they do respond with hostility, you shouldn't return the favor—instead, be calm and if needed, end the conversation and try to return to it at a later time.

Don't Get Manipulated

While being careful and gentle is a must in talking with a narcissist, it's also important that you don't get manipulated or exploited. Understand that narcissists are after admirers and not people who they could build strong relationships with. The ego is their fuel and you shouldn't get caught up with their praises and favors that you end up getting used. Keep this in mind and don't lose the focus on yourself when it comes with dealing with a narcissist.

Don't Get Abused by a Narcissist

Having a narcissist friend or partner is difficult, but it's also important that you don't allow yourself to be abused. Whether it's physically or psychologically, set ground rules in interacting with a narcissist and be frank when things start to get out of hand. If the narcissist tries to coerce you to do something that you don't want to do, tell it to him straight and just move on. Narcissists tend to lie and they lie a lot, so you also want to be straightforward about this in a gentle and calm manner, stating the facts and not dwelling on it further to promote a healthy and non-aggressive interaction with the narcissist.

Negotiating with a Narcissist

When it comes to negotiating and setting agreements, it can be hard with a narcissist. But the magic comes with goal setting in terms of interaction. Those with NPD cherish accomplishing things as this raises their self-worth and confidence, so set goals with the narcissist to provide a sense of pride for him while accomplishing a task. For example, if you have a narcissist partner who doesn't want to do the cooking, try urging him to host a house party or a special dinner for the family—this way, he or she has something to brag about once the task is accomplished while also achieving a positive outlook on the chore.

Helping Someone with NPD

Knowing how to deal with their behavior in the most positive way possible is key to promote self-actualization in narcissists in order for them to recognize their disruptive and irrational beliefs about themselves and see the world in a realistic way. Social interaction is where a narcissist feels strong and weak at the same time.

How to Deal with a Narcissist Partner

Having a narcissist partner is one of the biggest social challenges that you can face. You don't want them to be angry but you don't want to get manipulated all the time as well. In the face of a healthy relationship, you have to acknowledge that this narcissistic trait may be here to stay for a long time and you have to do coping that can promote a positive interaction between the two of you. Recognizing bad behavior like lying and setting goals are important in order to deal with a narcissist partner.

How to Deal with a Narcissist Parent

Having a narcissistic mom or dad can be difficult to deal with but it's a must to have a health relationship with parents. The most common problem with narcissistic parents is that they fail to recognize their mistakes and think that their child is talking back to them—a sign of disrespect. But in order to get past that barrier, you need to lay down ground rules and discuss the situation with them in a gentle and neutral manner. Negotiating is also a helpful tool in accomplishing goals for parents who have narcissistic tendencies.

How to Deal with a Narcissist Sibling

Having a narcissistic brother or sister is a fairly common thing. Most of the time, narcissistic siblings will fight for your parents' attention even if it takes them cheating or lying to get what they want. Stating your opinion and collaborating with them is the most effective way in dealing with them, but if they give a hostile or aggressive reaction, it is best to let them cool off first then talk it out at a later time.

How to Deal with a Narcissist Friends

Friends with narcissistic tendencies isn't something new. There are probably some of your friends who exhibit such behaviors. In order to deal with their narcissistic behavior, the first thing that you have to do is to ascertain your role as their friend. Since narcissists see people as their ego boosters, putting your foot down as an important person in their life will preserve their ego but at the same time highlight your role as someone that deserves to be respected.

How to Deal with a Narcissist Co-worker or Boss

The workplace is a different type of environment to encounter a narcissist but a fairly common one at that. If you meet with a co-worker or a boss with narcissistic tendencies, avoid direct confrontation and initiating arguments. The best approach is still to use a calm voice and a gentle tone, especially in pointing out subjects where you don't agree with them.

Chapter 14: Narcissism In Romantic Relationships

The facts of narcissistic behaviors do not stop with just family and friends, the most vulnerable of places narcissism is seen is within loving, romantic relationships. Usually just seen in one partner, there are times it is seen in both, making for a very unhealthy relationship as a whole. We are living in an ever increasing narcissistic world, with the "pay attention to me" mentality that is fueled by outside factors such as social media. With this increase, there are more and more people who dive head first into relationships with these individuals without knowing it at first. As a narcissist's true colors start to shine, that is when their significant other begins to realize they have fallen for one. The thing in romantic relationships is, you more than likely love that person, and do not want to leave them. Within this chapter we shall discuss how narcissism appears in the romantic setting, as well as how to deal with your narcissistic partner.

A romantic relationship with conceited individuals is often compared to being on a haunting roller coaster ride with Jekyll and Hyde, with intense highs and lows. The main reason we connect with people on a deeper level is to bond with others. But narcissists do not gain romantic relationships for this reason. They are usually unable to 100% feel love, and lack the capability to truly connect and form normal attachments with others. But when their entire sense of self is dependent of the admiration of others, they are in need of people. They view people as more of a commodity than actual human beings.

Narcissists are forever living with deep voids inside them. The only things that fill such voids are the temporary love and esteem that is stemmed from another. Those that are characterized as narcissists often say that they are never satisfied for long periods of time, always on a mission to find the temporary fix to fill whatever craving they have at the time.

Oblivious to the wants and needs of other people, they enter relationships in the attempt to fill their temporary desires. They often look for those that are always available for sex, can stroke their ego or whatever else they crave. Relationships with narcissistic individuals are often described in three phases, listed below.

The Over-evaluation Phase

When choosing their next "victim", people affected by narcissism pick those carefully, usually by status. Anyone who is attractive, popular, gifted in some way that suits their fancy, or rich are highly targeted. The bigger the status, the higher the value, at least as seen by a narcissist.

Once someone is chosen, narcissistic people get into a tunnel vision type of living, in the pursuit of whom they picked, they will represent themselves in the most perfect image possible. In this phase, they tend to be excessively caring and loving, giving their targets truckloads of attention and compliments that sweep their victims right off their feet, into their arms for the taking.

Narcissists in this stage are very euphoric, as if on cloud 9. They idolize their targets by speaking of them often, and have big hopes and dreams. They believe they have found their soul-mate. This is sadly the closest that narcissistic people get to feelings love. This would be classified as infatuation by many others who do not exhibit permanent narcissistic behaviors.

The Devaluation Phase

This phase is when a narcissists mark is wiped off and when their significant others start to really see their true colors and what they are made of. The shift of behaviors has said to been either gradual or practically overnight for some. The attention they once gave you is gone, substituted with silence. Days and weeks could go by and you do not hear from them. This leaves a narcissist's victim wondering where the heck they went wrong.

The thing about narcissists is, they become bored easily. This is because that never-ending void we talked about earlier, needs to be filled yet again by something new. They are addicted to that euphoric high from the over-evaluation phase. They believed you were special, but not they don't think you are, because why would their void still be there if you were?

The blaming game starts, as they become ever so moody and agitated at the slightest of things. In attempts to create distance between them and you, they give you the silent treatment, which often makes the targets cling a bit to the narcissist in an attempt to understand and mend the relationship. But the harder one clings, the harder they pull away, and as they do this, they treat the target like a punching bag, criticizing and blaming them for everything.

The targets become an emotional wreck, for their narcissist significant other has left the relationship for no apparent reason. They use your misery as food to feed off of. It is the same as getting fueled by your admiration; it is not seen much differently by them. Targets try their damnest to try to seek out the person they so profoundly fell in love with before the mask was removed, to no avail. The thing is, that kind, caring individual you once cared for never really existed. It was an act to secure you to supply them with the tools they needed to temporarily fill their void(s). Heartbreaking, isn't it?

Narcissists continually treat victims like pedals of a flower, chanting "I love you" and "I love you not" for as long as the victim of their careless acts allows them to do so. They will come in and out of your life indifferently, as if nothing happened, just to see you suffer as they lure you back in time and time again.

Either the narcissist finds another target to sink their teeth into, or you will get sick of fighting for someone that is psychotic and no longer fighting for you and leave.

The Discard Phase

It is quite the sight to watch the phases of a narcissist, and how they can change overnight, pulling away as you grasp harder. Once their supply from you has dried up, they are on to the next, leaving major havoc in their wake. It is quite the task, getting over the relationship that one had with a narcissist. Victims are left with a shattered self-image, and picking up the pieces from all the hurt that this person who doesn't have a real conscience left. Recovering from narcissistic relationships will be discussed in ….

It is important to be vigilant, and not fall back in the grasp of the narcissistic person you used to love, for there are chances they may return to feed off of you some more. Once free, triple lock the door to yourself, which includes cutting all ties. Otherwise, you can end up like the many people in situations where they go through these three phases over and over and over again. And trust me, it is not fun.

I loved a narcissistic individual for three and a half years of my life, and oh man, can I tell you that those three short years seemed like a decade at the very least. She was charming, affectionate, down to earth...there was nothing to not like about her! For a year out of the three we managed to make a 6 hour long distance relationship work, spectacularly well. For a narcissist, it was a great cover, not having to be around me so she could do whatever she pleased. The mask came off rather quickly when she moved to my city in with me. It was a euphoric couple months, it was great to have closed the gap on our distance. But, she started spending more and more late nights at her pathetic fast food job. She became more distant quickly, keeping her feelings in a lockbox that I no longer had the key to. I then began to catch on to her rapid lies and manipulations, which angered her each time I questioned her. The physical abuse that stemmed from her drug abusive rage to the emotional turmoil that she made me live through, it took awhile, but I finally decided to cut ties. Despite the love I had for her, I could no longer put up with the daily bullshit that overshadowed my life and our relationship due to her careless actions. I cut my losses with her over a year ago, and she still occasionally pokes around to see if she can dig a hole back into my life. It is important to not let their charm sway you, no matter their words and kind actions. It is usually a ploy.

After a lot of personal mending and self-reflection, I can say I loved a narcissistic monster. Everyday was a challenge, but I learned where lines should be drawn, how to build boundaries, and how to once again love the most important person in the world, myself.

Chapter 15: How Did The Narcissist Use You To Gratify Certain Needs?

Think for a moment and test your memory with these simple questions. They will serve as your own glaring, flashing red lights.

- Because of your youth/inexperience or emotionally vulnerable state, did your partner know he/she could control you?
- Did your partner believe that your physical appearance made them look superior to themselves and others?
- Did your partner constantly need an audience to share their even minutest accomplishment?
- Did your partner like to show you off and consider you a trophy spouse? (for men a gorgeous woman and for women a rich/handsome man)

- Did your partner need you around to witness or join in on their pursuits of excitement and adventure?

If this is the case with you, you may have noticed over time that your wants, needs and desires for excitement and adventure were never of any consequence to your partner.

How Did the Narcissist Devalue You?

There is a devaluation process with narcissistic partners. It begins when your partner realizes that you are indeed a mere mortal and not a god or goddess they fantasized you were. Since you are merely human you will never be their equal so you will not be able to relate and appreciate their extraordinary genius. (Sarcasm intended)

It begins with finding fault in you and the devaluation begins with asking if you can dress in a type of manner that is like a celebrity; or to change your hair style, or making condescending remarks about your opinions, ideas and intellectual pursuits. Sometimes they can be downright vicious with, "You're nothing but a fat, ugly and stupid slob." Ugly, but it happens. My personal story dealt with being considered being fat. I find a great deal of humor looking back at this because I'm still trying to figure out how a size 6 is considered fat. (Sarcasm intended)

By this time your partner will no longer have any feelings for you and may have started fooling around behind your back. Remember, they are always on the prowl for the next best thing. Since they are narcissistic they were never be able to love you and the commitment of following through with the real maintenance of a bonded relationship is not existent.

Chapter 16: Treatment Methods For Narcissistic Personality Disorder

Once you have persuaded your friend or loved one to visit a doctor and be assessed for a medical condition or personality disorder; you will want to know and understand the treatment options available.

The first stage in any treatment or diagnosis is to visit your health professional and seek their advice. They will, as already mentioned, perform a variety of tests and talk extensively about your history; medical and otherwise, before referring you to a mental health specialist to establish if you have a mental health issue or a personality disorder.

Once a diagnosis has been reached; whether confirmed or not, the treatment will depend upon the level of the narcissistic personality.

Reality Testing

An important test is finding out how much a sufferer has remained in touch with reality. If someone spends too much time in their fantasy world they may be unable to function properly in the real world. Equally someone with NPD may find that they are exceptionally impulsive or self-destructive; this can be a result of the feeling that they are always right and their way is the only way. Of course this route is likely to cause harm to themselves or to others and people who display these tendencies are often hospitalized to protect themselves.

Hospitalization

A stay in hospital is usually brief, to ensure the immediate threat has passed; however these types of narcissistic personalities will need a strong support structure and are likely to have regular outpatient appointments to monitor their process. This can be an important method of supporting those who have had their ego's shattered and have retreated into their own, private world. This can happen to those with NPD as, despite the feeling of being right all the time, there will be times when others prove them wrong and they do not know how to handle this. Outpatient care can provide the emotional and physical support needed to allow a sufferer to recover their ego and start the process again. It is not a cure, but a support mechanism.

However, it is not easy to treat someone with NPD! Their own delusion of grandeur can be coupled with the perceived shame of being ill to make them very derisive to those who attempt to treat them. This will be particular true of junior doctors who they will feel are not worthy to treat them. Only the highest ranking doctor in the hospital will be accepted! Medical professionals have to accept this part of their condition and work on the basis that they need to show respect and that they are aware that the patient has a high sense of self worth. However, this must be balanced against showing any sign of weakness when prescribing medical treatment, or, of providing any support to the patient's feelings of grandeur. It is a difficult path to walk! Possibly the best approach is to offer support and then confront their weaknesses one at a time.

Outpatient treatment also needs to be carefully monitored; it is very easy for a patient to simply stop attending the appointments. This will destroy the entire process and it will be necessary to start again; probably with a different therapist. Any NPD sufferer will be likely to quit if they face criticism; unfortunately this is part of the recovery process and will be expected. To combat this it is essential for a sufferer to have a strong support network that will pick him up and ensure he returns for the next session.

Psychotherapy

Most people who are diagnosed, or suspected of having narcissistic personality disorder will be referred to a psychotherapist. However, it is highly likely that they will be referred for a specific crisis or another ancillary symptom; this is to avoid directly confronting the NPD and inflating the ego and sense of self worth. However, at all times during treatment it is essential that the therapist keeps the narcissistic behavior in mind; they may have to appear to be superhuman to get through to the sufferer and help them to use their narcissistic feelings to overcome their issues.

The aim of this therapy, which can take years to complete, is to enable a sufferer to accept the following personality traits and even embrace them:

- Learn to build relationships with colleagues; as equals. This will allow a long term relationship.

- Understand the skills they actually possess, as opposed to the ones they dream they possess. Knowing what they are capable of will allow them to tolerate criticism and even failure. This will even allow them to learn from their mistakes and do better the next time.

- Gain an understanding of their feelings and understand how to control them in a variety of different situations.

- Acknowledge that issues can affect their self esteem but that they do not have to have a detrimental effect on their life or dreams. Anything which affects them directly can be overcome and, if it cannot, then it can be used to make them mentally stronger.

- Accept that not all their goals are realistic. From this they will be able to set goals and achievements which are possible and which conditions need to be met to ensure these goals are possible. They will then be able to aim for something that they can achieve and experience true joy at having reached a real target.

Group Therapy

It can be difficult for a therapist to know exactly when the right time is to refer their patient to group therapy sessions; these are likely to happen alongside the individual psychotherapy sessions. This part of the treatment may take the longest. Group therapy is designed to provide a better grounding for the sufferer and encourage them to have a healthy understanding of their own individual nature and that of those around them. This can help them revise their coping methods and learn to be more aware of others and their thoughts and feelings.

To achieve this, the therapist firstly needs to empathize with the sufferer and share the surprise and the pain regarding the fact that the group wish to confront their image of themselves. As the sufferer learns to accept this criticism, it will encourage them find a structured way to respond rather than become either, angry and defensive, or retreat into their own world. This method of educating someone with what responses are acceptable, rather than attempting to change their personality has become a very successful approach.

Prescription Drugs

At present, there are no prescription medicines which have been shown to have any effect on a personality disorder. This is likely to remain the same as an effective treatment method can never be completed without fully understanding the cause of this disorder.

However, if a sufferer displays symptoms such as depression or anxiety, it is possible to be prescribed anti-depressants to assist with dealing with these symptoms and allow the therapy and support sessions to deal with educating the sufferer in how to control their personality urges and acceptable responses.

Perhaps one of the most difficult parts of any treatment is getting a person suffering with NPD to stick with a treatment course. They are likely to think it is beneath them and not worth their time; it will certainly not fit with their grandiose plans or feelings of importance! It is likely to be most difficult to stick to the treatment regime once they begin to get criticized or challenged. To assist with the treatment it is important to remind them of their goals and the importance of the following items:

- Treatment can be rewarding and open new opportunities; keep an open mind and they may be surprised at the results.

- The treatment plan is there for a reason! If they stick to it, even when it seems very difficult to, there will be a variety of rewards and the ultimate prize of a better balanced life.

- Educating themselves is crucial; as with any project the more they know the easier it is. Someone receiving treatment for NPD should learn all they can about narcissistic personalities and the different treatment options. Not only will they be able to understand the treatment and what is likely to occur, but they will also gain knowledge about the condition and this will help to re-enforce the principle that their disorder is not a personal failure.

- Should they be experiencing any substance abuse it is essential to obtain help for this at the same time; or possibly even before the treatment session starts. If this is not dealt with then they will simply start a cycle of unhealthy behavior and treatment; which will not benefit anyone.

- Relaxation is important. One of the triggers that someone with NPD will experience is the stress involved when their opinion is challenged. Learning to relax, possibly by gaining some yoga or tai chi knowledge will allow them to remain calm when they would not react aggressively. This can be a valuable help in stopping the cycle of grand dreams and deep emotion retreats.

- It is important for someone with NPD to know they are achieving their goals and, rather than having one big goal to aim for, it is best to break this down into as many smaller goals as possible and celebrate each little success. To start with, this may even be as simple as turning up for the therapy sessions! Keeping a sufferer motivated will be a valuable assistance in achieving their ultimate goal; of being a valued part of society.

It is important to remember that everyone is different and the approach to treatment will be unique to the individual. It should be discussed in detail with the sufferer, their medical professional and at least one member of their support group. As already mentioned, the aim is to educate someone; this is currently the best form of long term treatment.

Chapter 17: Is There Any Hope Of Treatment?

Narcissistic Personality Disorder

There is some hope that people with this pathology can be made aware of their symptoms, with clinical help. But it must be emphasized that there is no cure for the disorder. There no magic pill and there is no course of therapy which can eliminate the disorder from people who have NPD.

That said, hospitalization can have some mitigating effect on behavior, but in almost all cases, this is temporary. Further, hospitalization cannot be achieved without patient consent, which makes it exceedingly difficult to achieve, due to the lack of symptomatic awareness in NPD people. Hospitalization usually occurs in the event the patient suffers from a mental health co-morbidity (additional disorder, frequently histrionic personality disorder, borderline personality disorder, or obsessive compulsive disorder), or is self-destructive, compelling physician recommendation that hospitalization occur.

Successful hospitalization should be attended by intensive psychotherapy which seeks to improve the social function of the patient. In this way, the process serves more than a "containment" function, providing the patient with the possibility of finding ways, with the help of mental health professionals, to mitigate destructive and recurrent behaviors.

While NPD may not be cured, there is hope that, through intensive therapeutic intervention, patients may lead more normal lives and have an enhanced ability to form lasting friendships and relationships, as well as to sustain employment more effectively. Central to therapeutic intervention is the clinician's ability to instill in the patient a readier acknowledgement of reality, without exacerbating the sense of insecurity and low self-esteem generally found to be the root cause of NPD. Replacing an inappropriately inflated sense of self-worth arising as a coping mechanism with a realistic self-assessment is key to therapy's effectiveness.

Anti-Social Personality Disorder (Sociopathy)

Unlike NPD, there is very little evidence to suggest that sociopaths may be helped through therapeutic intervention, unless the disorder is identified in childhood. But therapists are unwilling to diagnose ASPD in the young, as the personality has not yet fully developed. This presents a challenge to therapists hoping to find methods by which the proliferation of sociopathic behavior might be stemmed.

There is no known medication that can cope with the disorder.

The only forms of therapy which have been proven to show limited success in confrontation of sociopathy are intensive programs which encompass every sector of the patient's life. There is a logistical challenge in this approach which is obvious, as every person the sociopath interacts with must be fully engaged in the project of mitigating the destructive and aberrant behavior involved in this pathology. Because adults are free agents, this methodology is futile, as adult patients must consent and because of the nature of sociopathy, this is highly unlikely to happen.

In short, there is no known treatment for full blown, adult sociopathy, to date. As for children with the disorder, the programmatic demands and the reticence of mental health professionals to diagnosis children with the pathology, makes it unlikely that sociopaths can be treated at all, in the prevailing context. This means the only known way to reduce the impact of this pathology when it appears in our lives, is to either cut off all contact, or employ the strategies enumerated above. Mitigating impact is the only way we can protect ourselves from the social menace represented by ASPD.

Chapter 18: To Be Narcissistic Is "In"

Another factor that greatly contributes to a child's personality formation is the overuse of television in the early years as well as the imitation mechanisms that play a major role in the development of what an image is in the child's mind. In order to understand such an idea better, we simply need to consider the consequences and the negative impact that different Tv protagonists or "stars" have on children that steadily urge them to dress and act just like their "idols". The position that parents take towards those matters is equally important as well, since this early identification with the Tv personalities which develops in imitation later on is usually addressed towards their face. It is, therefore, understandable that the parent's example, the values, disciplines and their morals mirror the way that they

163

want to raise their children and set the rules and regulations for their upbringing. The result, however, of the increasing focus and occupation with the children's appearance may be the reason why the children fail to develop new skills and to invest in human relations. This is when the parents need to emphasize the importance of education, mental cultivation, participation in challenging activities and empowerment of the children's socialization. In a society that demands the children to be self-centered, self-absorbed and self-made as a whole, it is important for them to understand the inner satisfaction helping others, donating and being open to receive new ideas and concepts brings. If children fail to internalize those simple principles, they are much more likely to end up being narcissistic beings simply because they have not been in contact with any helpful concepts that would better their personalities.

The beginning of adolescence signals the entrance in a new phase of life, full of not only physical changes but also psychological turbulence that can lead to new alterations as much as to the way of thinking as to the way the teenagers behave. This also means that the adolescent is taken over by new emotions such as agony, fears and worries, which he is called to handle and reclaim in a way that helps him evolve as a person. Moreover, a teenager's relationship with the opposite sex as well as the image he projects to his peers seem to monopolize his daily reality. For these reasons, teenagers become more and more interested in their appearance and in how acceptable they are by their peers, who they wish to associate with in an effort to understand themselves, share thoughts and feelings and to experience the feeling of "belonging somewhere" which is established around this age. By observing a teenager, one can easily see the changes that occur periodically not only on his physical appearance but also on the abrupt emotional transitions as a result of the constant experimentation in the quest to establish a unique identity, but in the end all teens share a common pattern of continuously adapting to new looks and trends, taking care of himself, tending to impress, imitate, risk and try. Consequently, it is that era when all narcissistic tendencies and signs are more intense than ever.

Chapter 19: The 9 Most Common Symptoms Of Narcissistic Personality Disorder

1. Self-Important

One of the more obvious signs of Narcissistic Personality Disorder is the belief that one is extremely important compared to others. They will see themselves as having a higher level of importance and will exaggerate this importance. Bragging, exaggerating their worth, and focusing a great deal on the aspects they think are significant, can make this symptom very apparent. The person will often belittle others because they see no reason not to. In their eyes, they are already more important and superior and so they see no problem in pointing it out or expecting this to be common knowledge. Nothing in particular has to occur or be present for the person to see themselves this way. They already have the thought cemented in their mind and little can be done to dissuade them. When in a group, they will often push to be the center of attention, or walk away with the expectation that they will be followed. They will assume that people will do as they are told or will instantly respect them for what they say and do. For whatever reasons, the idea of them being much more important is something they see no challenge or opposing views in. [2]

2. Delusion

With Narcissistic Personality Disorder, they often live in a dream or false reality. This is kind of an overall issue as it puts all the other symptoms together in a synthetic world. Most of their beliefs are falsified in their own mind. This, in turn, allows a screen to cover everything around them in order to color the world in such a way that they find themselves having a significance that normally would not exist. The delusion is then set to allow for someone to see this imagined reality as an allowance for their arrogance. Often this can play out in such a way that the person will have people that do abide by their assumed superiority, giving credence to the false reality, and thus making the symptoms and the disorder more difficult to dispute. The false reality also acts as a protective barrier for a narcissist who is this way due to childhood trauma or abuse. Creating a world in which they are above what they have experienced, are better because of what they have gone through, or a reality completely separate from the one they actually had is their way of coping. If a person has suffered in such a way that they have decided upon a world in which better things happened to them and they came out on top, it can seem difficult to change this state of mind. In truth, it can also be rather dangerous.

This false world does allow the person to have overbearing behavior and unrealistic beliefs about themselves, but it also protects them from the mental damage and scarring of acknowledging or even experiencing what they have actually lived through. [2]

3. Finicky Standards

Narcissists believe that they can only be understood by and able to communicate with people they think are as exceptional as they are. This drastically lessens the number of people they think are even worth talking to. Being that they use inflated sense of self to confirm their personal ideas of who they are, they will not have any issue with people who do the same. On top of that is the idea that if someone is as exceptional as they are, they strive to surpass this person in order to prove their own self-worth. Being overly selective of such similar people will, again, add to the haughtiness they give off. Because the person is selective without knowing why they are selective, those whom they see as below them will obviously be shunned or feel humiliated for not being equal to the narcissist. [2]

4. High Expectations

Narcissistic Personality Disorder will leave the person demanding more from others. They will come to expect the admiration and honor they believe they deserve. Offense is easily taken at anyone who does not bow to them and their believed superiority. If they are able to scam or take advantage of someone, they will continue to do so because they feel that if they did it once, then they must do it every time in order to keep up the appearance they originally set forth. The idea of demanding more is a way to confirm their authority or higher position over the people around them. They do not see a problem in expecting more and, in fact, may see a person as better for adhering to their growing needs and expectations. Though the people that endure this constant and ever-growing demand may see themselves as less for bending to the will of someone they may even consider as underserving of their help, the narcissist will rarely notice any growing resentment. In their narcissistic delusion, people will want to help them because they want to be affiliated with a person as great as they are. [2]

5. Demanding Special Treatment

Favoritism and immediate compliance is an automatic expectation from people around someone with Narcissistic Personality Disorder. They expect their treatment to be above that of anyone else and see no reason for this to ever be different. They assume they can get away with more and often do simply because people are either afraid of them, annoyed by them, or just want them to be happy and get rid of them. With the compliance of those dealing with the narcissist, the special treatment becomes an expectation. This leads to them constantly expecting more each time. Giving in to someone's preference, though, does not always mean they are doing it out of kindness or bowing down to people with this level of arrogance and sense of self. More often than not, it is the way to be rid of the person who is demanding such treatment. The narcissist can utilize annoyance by being overly persistent. Though this makes others comply with their fantasy of superiority, it does satisfy their idea of being better. So what you end up with is someone with Narcissistic Personality Disorder demanding something they expect out of someone, receiving it and consistently asking for more which causes that person to resent the narcissist and complies in order to be rid of them. The narcissist still sees it as submission to their perceived mental hierarchy and accepts the acquiescence even if it is not in a subservient way. [2]

6. Exploiting Others

Exploitation, or using others for their own gain, is another symptom of Narcissistic Personality Disorder. Narcissists find that other people are easier to take advantage of because such people either conform to their idea of being more superior or others bend to their will strictly because of how everyone else sees and treats them highly. Having a sense of being better and smarter than everyone, it is easy for someone with this disorder to use people for their own benefit. In their eyes, these people are not worthy to be respected and as such, it seems reasonable to use them to their benefit. Again we have a symptom that connects to other symptoms quite simply. Exploitation comes from their belief that they are owed what they are demanding and they will constantly demand more. They then see these people that adhere to their domineering personality as below them or less important because they can be exploited. [2]

7. Lack of Empathy

Empathy is something that narcissists usually lack. Their inability to understand and feel what others feel makes them incapable of relating to others. This further goes back to the idea that they are better than everyone else. Just as many people see animals as less intelligent and thus easier to treat however they want to treat them, the same goes with someone with Narcissistic Personality Disorder. They do not see people around them as being smart enough to have the level of thinking and emotions that they do, so they ignore the importance of those emotions and feelings. This allows a numbing effect which gives way to other symptoms, like exploitation. [2]

8. Envy

The insecurities from which Narcissistic Personality Disorder are based creates jealousy and envy in such people. It can also be true that they think others are just as envious of them as they are of other people. There is anger at anyone who has proof of actually being better or more successful and so they are angry that they too do not have this same proof and glaring evidence of their own heightened level amongst others. Envy is a core feeling and thus it is one of the rawest feelings a narcissist can have. For them, nothing is worse than realizing they are not as great as they think or say and that there are others that are. This conflicts with the idea of their superiority and they have a hard time processing it. Envy does not merge well with the façade they have created. In order to preserve their ideas without revealing their insecurities, they turn their envy into resentment. This leads to higher levels of accosting toward the party they are envious of. The threats, criticisms, and harsh words could be the beginning of a very dark cycle. This symptom is extremely prevalent with grandiose personality types. [2]

9. Arrogance

The number one most evident feature of Narcissistic Personality Disorder is arrogance. The idea of superiority and high standings leave the person feeling better in a multitude of ways. This leads to the arrogance, or haughtiness, that comes with narcissism. The smug looks, pretentious tones, smirks of disdain, and so on, show their disbelief of anyone else's importance while accentuating their own.

Arrogance is the basis of most of the narcissist's actions. Arrogance is also a result of the reactions of the people they exploit, see as below or less than them, and the purposeful interactions with people of a higher standing (of whom they see a common importance with). The cycle is brutal in this way. Arrogance and self-importance creates the false reality in which they believe they are better than everyone else, which leads to how they treat and see others, which then leads into a greater arrogance. [2]

Chapter 20: Can You Deal With A Narcissist? Tips And Strategies

What if you don't have any codependent traits, but you simply come across narcissists and you have to deal with them? Maybe your coworker is a narcissist. It can also happen that your very boss is a narcissist ... which is of course quite delicate and complicated. Maybe you have a narcissistic mother-in-law. Maybe you simply want to learn a few strategies and be well equipped whenever you encounter such a person.

First of all, you have to stand your ground, no matter whom you're dealing with. If you show you have strong boundaries, but no hostility towards the narcissist, you can manage to keep relatively peaceful relationships without being abused. By no means should you allow anyone to bully you, order you around, or make demands that are far-fetched and inappropriate. If the narcissist is not a coworker, your boss, or a close family member, just discard them at the first red flags. You can always find a new partner, new friends, and more fun. However, life is not always so easy and you may actually have to deal with a family member or someone who is a professional position of superiority. What do you do in such a case if you want to keep good relationships and your job, but also avoid falling prey to narcissistic abuse?

If you're dealing with someone at work, make sure most discussions take place in a group setting. Otherwise, the narcissist may steal your ideas or treat you badly if there's no social pressure. Narcissists usually don't care too much and have no sense of shame, but they do want to keep an image that allows for many followers and admirers. This means a group setting is not the perfect context for exerting overt narcissistic abuse. Try to set boundaries as much as possible if the boss or a colleague tries to pressure you into taking on extra workload (for no money). Similarly, stick to your own duty only if they try to throw responsibility and blame on you. It's self-understood that an extremely unhealthy or corrupt environment should compel you to leave and look for another job. A narcissistic boss is not easy to deal with, especially if they think you are not irreplaceable and they have no authentic respect for your skills. If the person only tries to push your boundaries and see how much you can take and if you can be exploited, stand your ground and show you know what you want. Also subtly show what you cannot accept. If you see the person is really determined to abuse you by any means and they have social and professional power over you, maybe you should consider finding a better job instead of strategies to deal with the narcissist.

For other cases in which you can maintain your boundaries and your power, you can consider getting the upper hand and making the narcissist depend on you. For instance, this may be possible with a coworker or a relative. Show you have some precious knowledge or expertise the narcissist needs. Make subtle promises that you could also teach them how to master it. Show no weakness, avoid expressing emotion in front of them, and do your best to appear invulnerable, but also friendly. Don't share any personal information about yourself or your relationships with the narcissist. At the first signs of NPD, you should simply place that person in the right (medical) category and treat them with extreme caution. Remember that narcissists can be charismatic and ingenious when they want to get under your skin. It's essential to keep in mind how to recognize symptoms of narcissism in order to stay out of further trouble. Your only aim should be making yourself untouchable by the narcissist's egotistic needs and tentacles and keeping a neutral relationship.

Similarly, when dealing with a relative, you can act in a way that shows strength, self-control, but also something they find desirable. For instance, you could flatter the narcissistic relative occasionally or bring them a gift. That would make them stay relatively peaceful towards you or at least not hate you. When dealing with a relative you probably have all the interest to avoid conflict. Never criticize the person, but don't allow them to feed their ego with you, either. The key is staying clean and desirable. This way you can manipulate the narcissist a bit instead of having them maneuver and exploit you. Don't respond to their emotional needs and don't allow the relationship to fall into anything else. For instance, if your narcissistic sister-in-law tries to become 'friends' and wants to start visiting you by herself, do your best to avoid that. If you have NPD red flags already, you should know she probably only wants to trap you and maybe charge you with a few of her problems and flaws. Keep extremely clear relationships boundaries. A narcissistic coworker or relative should never have the opportunity to become something else. If you give in to their attempts at getting closer, you will likely regret it later.

When you find yourself on the verge of getting caught in the scripts the narcissist has in their own head, make sure you have a means of exit at hand. Keep your eyes open and be alert. Check everything they say against facts and never let the narcissist use you as a garbage bin for their projections. If you really have to (say, you're having Christmas dinner with your relative), you can listen to one or two of their self-centered stories and nod to maintain peace. However if you see signs of aggression and abuse towards you and you feel the pressure of their projections, find your way out immediately. Set boundaries, maintain an explicit identity, and change the topic immediately.

For instance, the narcissist may attempt to get rid of a few complexes and put you down by insinuating you changed your job because you weren't good enough. Let's say the events in your life are not clear enough: why did you change your job after all? The narcissist doesn't really know what happened, but in their arrogance and need for superiority, they are likely to suggest you didn't feel competent enough, your boss told you to leave etc. What should you do? First of all, don't get defensive. Keep calm and bring a few provable facts in the discussion (e.g. you had applied for a better job a while before; you had a new diploma which allowed you to look for something more suitable etc.). Just state that information without any emotional connotations or additions. By no means should you let the narcissist make you angry with their assumptions or allusions. Then start speaking enthusiastically about your new job a bit. Simply stand your ground and keep your own frame of reference without being fazed. Smile and joke at will. Change the topic to something less personal afterwards. You should aim at staying away from narcissistic projection and abuse as well as at avoiding conflict. Insert one of two compliments for the narcissist's real or illusory qualities to avoid angering them or having them feel defeated. Remember that answering overtly to the narcissist's provocation will only escalate conflict. A narcissist needs social reassurance, not being openly defeated in competition or a battle of wits.

When you have to deal with a narcissist at work, make sure you never personalize anything and focus on tasks and solutions to any problems that may come up. The narcissist is likely to try to charm you into revealing weaknesses or personal information. Be sly and subtle without literally trying to one-up them. Try to divert their attention by bringing up 'safe' topics. For instance, you can comment on the brand of their clothes ('wow, this coat looks terrific on you! Where did you find such a wonderful thing?'). You can bring up a film or an event in town ('have you been to that expensive club yet? you probably have ...knowing you!'). Alternatively talk about a tangential professional issue that is not likely to make them envious ('I've just discovered this new book that could help us both in this project; let me know if you want me to lend it to you!'). There are many ways of distracting the narcissist from your own personality or life. Keep communication as neutral and professional as possible while also reassuring the narcissist of your good intentions, namely your disinterest in competing with them or threatening their position. Needless to say, if you talk about your achievements too much, you are likely to anger them. Therefore, it may be safer to keep some of them well hidden from the narcissist unless it's really something you must inevitably talk about such as your PhD or your promotion.

Last, but not least, listen a lot and try to be as constructive as possible. Avoid getting entangled in mind games or ego trips (unless you're also a narcissist and you can't help it!). Try to humanize the narcissist without idealizing them in any way. What does this mean? Well, you could try to be understanding and tolerant of their disorder, if you have to deal with them. Remember that more often than not narcissists have deep-seated wounds and pools of insecurity that engendered their disorder. Use your own persuasive powers to negotiate with the narcissist in a way that suggests mutual benefit. Without getting manipulative, just try to make it obvious to them that they could benefit from keeping peace with you and not trying to abuse or exploit you. The key is staying nonreactive to their games, maintaining independence, and reassuring them you don't want to harm or one-up them. You don't have to try to please them – that will likely make them take you for an easy prey! However let them think they are in control as long as that doesn't endanger your position and doesn't mean some form of abuse. You can freely nod and listen to them as they brag once or twice to make them feel secure, but make sure that doesn't become a bad habit or a relational pattern.

Additionally, you can stay as elusive as possible while trying to get a lot of insight into the narcissist's mind. Discover what makes them tick (so that you can use it just in case) while staying impenetrable and impersonal yourself. Narcissists are accustomed to see people in black and white terms and to objectify them. If you let yourself be pinned down, they will mentally place you in a category right away and use all their weapons against you. They surely have enough experience and practice! So make yourself invulnerable and unreadable while maintaining an air of friendliness and safety.

Chapter 21: How To Reverse The Roles

Why not switch roles? You can turn the tables so quickly and make your manipulative, lying abuser taste her own medicine. This is a good way to teach women to not mess with you. Proving that you can play games too can intimidate women and make them stop right away.

The only problem with playing games like this is that you make yourself no better than the liars, cheaters, and con artists in your life. If this fact does not bother you, then you should proceed. But carefully consider if you really want to reverse the roles. It is sometimes better to just walk away from a manipulator or liar, and not stoop to her immature and abusive level.

However, the temptation to get revenge is sometimes far too enticing. You can teach someone a lesson by flipping the tables on her and using her own methods against her. She will not like it one bit. She will probably leave you alone, or else she will realize that she has been full of shit and she will clean up her act. Either way, you can achieve a lot by reversing roles on an emotional abuser.

How can you reverse the roles? It can be hard to do this, especially if you are not a manipulative jerk yourself. You come from a victim's standpoint, not a perpetrator's. But you can learn a few tricks that can help you reverse the roles and gain the lead.

Don't Play Into Games

When a woman plays a game in an attempt to get you jealous or guilty, understand what she wants. Then refuse to give it to her.

Say a woman throws a fit and plays the "Fine, I won't go" game in order to get you to come along to an event that you have no desire to attend. Shut this game down immediately by saying, "OK." Don't plead with her to go or ask her to reconsider. Don't agree to go along with her, either. You have the right to say no and make your own choices, so don't give in to her little guilt trips.

When a woman tries to make you jealous, don't ever admit to any jealousy or do what she wants. Instead, try to make her jealous. Point out another woman that you find hot. She will realize how bad it feels to be the victim of the jealousy game.

Undermine all of a woman's manipulative games. She will hate it. You will make her feel powerless when you refuse to play along with the games that she is used to getting her way with.

Reverse Psychology

Tell a woman the opposite of what you want her to do. Mention what you do want her to do so that the idea is planted in her mind. Then, when she resists, suggest that you didn't really want her to do that anyway. She will begin to want to act on this planted idea just to irritate you. Little does she know that she is actually doing exactly what you wanted. You can find extra success with this in bed when you want her to do things that she would normally refuse to do.

Offer Consequences

Manipulators will withhold love from you to punish you when you don't do just what they want. You can play the same game. If someone does anything you don't like – lies to you, cheats on you – confront her. Then offer her a punishment. You can withhold sex or you can give her the silent treatment. You can even threaten to leave her. Use the same punishment that she likes to use on you. She will hate it and she will realize how awful her little punishments are.

Be Selfish for Once

A manipulator is probably taking advantage of you. When she needs your help with something, you are there. When she wants to talk, you listen. Yet you never get anything back. When you call on her for help, she turns her phone off or says that she is busy, sorry!

For once, you should be the selfish one. Don't do anything for her. When she asks you for a favor or starts to vent to you, just say that you are too tired and you want to go to bed. Always demand that she does something for you before you do anything for her. She will be floored that you are not bending over backward for her as usual, and she will probably flip out.

Level her with Accusations

When she starts accusing you of things, immediately counteract that by leveling your own accusations against her. These accusations can be real or they can be entirely made up. Either way, accusing her of things will very quickly flip the argument on its head. She will jump to her defenses and will let go of whatever problem she has with you. You can also condition her to stop bringing up the same things over and over again because you will show her that every time she mentions the same old argument, you will bring up your own same old argument too.

Make her Feel Guilty

Use guilt against her. When she starts her old antics, use something that she did in the past against her. For instance, if she starts accusing you of cheating, bring up the inappropriate texts that you found on her phone months ago. Bring up old problems and resolved past conflicts to get her to back off. Women love to play this game, but we are not used to men turning it on us. No woman will enjoy hearing about old stuff after it has been hashed out and resolved.

CPSIA information can be obtained
at www.ICGtesting.com
Printed in the USA
LVHW011028110121
676044LV00007B/277